新丝路"中文+职业技能"系列教材编写委员会
（中文+计算机网络技术）

总策划：马箭飞　谢永华
策　划：宋永波　孙雁飞
顾　问：朱志平（北京师范大学）
　　　　林秀琴（首都师范大学）
　　　　宋继华（北京师范大学）

总主编：谢永华　杜曾慧
语言类主编：朱金兰
专业类主编：周　惠
语言类副主编：刘欣娟　孙世娟
专业类副主编：廖常武　黄　珏　尧海昌
专业类参编：岳兆新

项目组长：郭凤岚
项目副组长：付彦白
项目成员：郭　冰　武传霞　齐　琰　赫　栗　李金梅

 新丝路"中文+职业技能"系列教材
New Silk Road "Chinese + Vocational Skills" Series

中文+计算机网络技术

Chinese + Computer Networking Technology

中级 Intermediate

新丝路"中文+职业技能"系列教材编写委员会　编

© 2024 北京语言大学出版社，社图号 23195

图书在版编目 (CIP) 数据

中文＋计算机网络技术．中级／新丝路"中文＋职业技能"系列教材编写委员会编．－－北京：北京语言大学出版社，2024.1

新丝路"中文＋职业技能"系列教材

ISBN 978-7-5619-6416-3

Ⅰ．①中… Ⅱ．①新… Ⅲ．①汉语－对外汉语教学－教材②计算机网络－教材　Ⅳ．① H195.4 ② TP393.08

中国国家版本馆 CIP 数据核字（2023）第 239172 号

中文＋计算机网络技术（中级）
ZHONGWEN + JISUANJI WANGLUO JISHU (ZHONGJI)

排版制作：	北京创艺涵文化发展有限公司
责任印制：	周　燚

出版发行：	北京语言大学出版社
社　　址：	北京市海淀区学院路 15 号，100083
网　　址：	www.blcup.com
电子信箱：	service@blcup.com
电　　话：	编 辑 部 8610-82303647/3592/3724
	国内发行 8610-82303650/3591/3648
	海外发行 8610-82303365/3080/3668
	北语书店 8610-82303653
	网购咨询 8610-82303908
印　　刷：	北京富资园科技发展有限公司

版　　次：	2024 年 1 月第 1 版	**印　次：**	2024 年 1 月第 1 次印刷
开　　本：	889 毫米 × 1194 毫米 1/16	**印　张：**	11
字　　数：	202 千字		
定　　价：	98.00 元		

PRINTED IN CHINA

凡有印装质量问题，本社负责调换。售后 QQ 号 1367565611，电话 010-82303590

编写说明

新丝路"中文+职业技能"系列教材是把中文作为第二语言,结合专业和职业的专门用途、职业用途的中文教材,不是专业理论教材,不是一般意义的通用综合中文教材。本系列教材定位为职场生存中文教材、立体式技能型语言教材。教材研发的目标是既要满足学习者一般中文环境下的基本交际需求,又要满足学习者职业学习需求和职场工作需求。它和普通的国际中文教材的区别不在语法,而在词汇的专门化程度,在中文的用途、使用场合、应用范围。目前,专门用途、职业用途的中文教材在语言分类和研究成果上几近空白,本系列教材的成功研发开创了中文学习的新视野、新领域、新方向,将"中文+职业技能+X等级证书"真正融合,使学习者在学习中文的同时,也可通过实践掌握职业技能,从而获得X等级证书。

适用对象

本系列教材将适用对象定位为双零基础(零语言基础、零技能基础)的来华学习中文和先进技能的长期或者短期进修生,可满足初、中、高各层次专业课程的教学需要。教材亦可供海内外相关的培训课程及"走出去"的中资企业培训本土化员工使用。

结构规模

本系列教材采取专项语言技能与职业技能训练相结合的中文教学及教材编写模式。教材选择当前热门的物流管理、汽车服务工程技术、电子商务、机电一体化、计算机网络技术、酒店管理等六个专业,培养各专业急需急用的技术岗位人才。每个专业教材均包括初、中、高级三册。每一册都配有专业视频教学资源,还附有"视频脚本""参考答案"等配套资源。

编写理念

本系列教材将词语进行分类,区分普通词语和专业词语,以通用语料为基础,以概念性、行为性词语为主,不脱离职场情境讨论分级,做到控制词汇量,控制工作场景,控制交流内容与方式,构建语义框架。将语言的分级和专业的分级科学地融合,是实现本系列教材成功编写的关键。

教材目标

语言技能目标:

初级阶段,能熟练掌握基础通用词语和职场的常用专业词语,能使用简短句子进行简单的生活及工作交流。中级阶段，能听懂工作场合简单的交谈与发言，明白大意，把握基本情况，能就工作中重要的话题用简单的话与人沟通。高级阶段，能听懂工作场合一般的交谈与发言，抓住主要内容和关键信息，使用基本交际策略与人交流、开展工作，能初步了解与交际活动相关的文化因素，掌握与交际有关的一般文化背景知识，能排除交际时遇到的文化障碍。交际能力层次的递进实现从初级的常规礼节、基本生活及工作的交流能力，到中级的简单的服务流程信息交流能力，最后达到高级的复杂信息的交流和特情处理的能力。

职业技能目标：

以满足岗位需求为目标，将遴选出的当前热门的专业工作岗位分为初、中、高三级。物流管理专业初、中、高级对应的岗位分别是物流员、物流经理、物流总监；汽车服务工程技术专业初、中、高级对应的岗位分别是汽车机电维修工、汽车服务顾问、技术总监；电子商务专业初、中、高级对应的岗位分别是电子商务运营助理、电子商务运营员、电子商务客服；机电一体化专业初、中、高级对应的岗位分别是机电操作工、机电调整工、机电维修工；计算机网络技术专业初、中、高级对应的岗位分别是宽带运维工程师、网络运维专员、网络管理员；酒店管理专业初、中、高级对应的岗位分别是前厅基层接待员、前厅主管、前厅经理。每个专业分解出三十个工作场景/任务，学习者在学习后能够全面掌握此岗位的概况及基本程序，实现语言学习和专业操作的双重目标。

编写原则

1. 语言知识技能与专业知识技能并进，满足当前热门的、急需急用的岗位需求。

2. 渐进分化，综合贯通，拆解难点，分而治之。

3. 语言知识与专业知识科学、高效复现，语言技能与专业技能螺旋式上升，职场情境、语义框架、本体输入方式相互配合。

4. 使用大量的图片和视频，实现专业知识和技能呈现形式可视化。

5. 强化专业岗位实操性技能。本系列教材配有专业技术教学的视频，突出展示专业岗位的实操性技能，语言学习难度与技能掌握难度的不匹配可通过实操性强的视频和实训环节来补充。

特色追求

本系列教材从初级最基础的语音知识学习和岗位认知开始，将"中文+职业技能"融入在工作场景对话中，把工作分解成一个个任务，用图片认知的方式解决专业词语的认知问题，用视频展示的方法解决学习者掌握中文词语与专业技能的不匹配问题，注重技能的实操性，注重"在做中学"。每一单元都设置了"学以致用"板块，目的不仅仅是解决本单元任务的词语认知问题，更是将学习的目标放在"能听""能用""能模仿说出"上。我们力争通过大量图片的使用和配套视频的展示，将教材打造成立体式、技能型语言教材，方便学习者能够更好地自主学习。

使用建议

1. 本系列教材每个专业分为初、中、高级三册，每册10单元，初级每单元建议8～10课时完成，中级10～12课时完成，高级12～14课时完成。

2. 教材注释和说明着力于简明扼要，注重实操性，注重听说技能培养，对于教材涉及的语法知识，教师可视情况予以细化和补充。

3. "单元实训"板块可以在课文和语言点学完之后作为课堂练习使用，建议2课时完成。教师要带着学习者按照实训步骤一步步完成，实训步骤不要求学习者能够看懂，读懂，重要的是教师要引领操作，实现学习者掌握专业技能的目标。

4. "单元小结"板块是对整个单元关键词语和核心内容的总结，对于这部分内容，教师要进行听说练习，以便更好地帮助学习者了解本单元的核心工作任务。

5. 教师上课时要充分利用教材设计的练习，引导学习者多听多练，听说结合，学做合一。

6. 教师要带着学习者熟练诵读课文，要求学习者把每课的关键词语和句子、课堂用语背诵下来。

特别感谢

感谢教育部中外语言交流合作中心将新丝路"中文＋职业技能"系列教材列为重点研发项目，为我们教材编写增添了动力和责任感。教材编写委员会负责整套教材的规划、设计与编写协调，并先后召开上百次讨论会，对每册教材的课文编写、体例安排、注释说明、练习设计、图片选择、视频制作等进行全方位的评估、讨论和审定。感谢编写委员会成员和所有编者高度的敬业精神、精益求精的编写态度，以及所投入的热情和精力、付出的心血与智慧。感谢关注本系列教材并贡献宝贵意见的国际中文教育教学界专家和全国各地的同人。

新丝路"中文＋职业技能"系列教材编写委员会
2023年4月

Compilation Instructions

The New Silk Road "Chinese + Vocational Skills" is a series of Chinese textbooks for specialized and vocational purposes that combine professional and vocational technologies with Chinese as a second language. Instead of being specialized theoretical textbooks, or comprehensive or universal Chinese textbooks in a general sense, this series is intended to be Chinese textbooks for career survival, and three-dimensional skills-based language textbooks. The textbooks are developed with a view to meeting students' basic communication needs in general Chinese environment, and their professional learning needs and workplace demands as well. They are different from ordinary Chinese textbooks for foreigners in the degree of specialization of vocabulary, in the purpose, usage occasion, and application scope of Chinese (not in grammar). At present, Chinese textbooks for specialized and vocational purposes are virtually non-existent in terms of language classification and research results, so the successful development of this series has opened up new horizons, new fields and new directions for Chinese learning, and virtually integrated "Chinese + Vocational Skills + X-Level Certificates", which enables students to practically master vocational skills and obtain X-level certificates while learning Chinese.

Applicable Targets

This series is targeted at long-term or short-term students who come to China to learn Chinese and advanced skills with zero language basis and zero skill basis, which can meet the teaching needs of the elementary, intermediate and advanced specialized courses. This series can also be used for relevant training courses at home and abroad and for Chinese-funded enterprises that "go global" to train local employees.

Structure and Scale

This series adopts a Chinese teaching and textbook compilation model combining special language skills and vocational skills training. The series includes the textbooks for six popular majors such as logistics management, automotive service engineering technology, e-commerce, mechatronics, computer networking technology, and hotel management to cultivate technical talents in urgent need. The textbooks for each major consist of the textbooks at the elementary, intermediate and advanced levels. Each textbook is equipped with professional video teaching resources, and "video scripts", "reference answers" and other supporting resources as well.

Compilation Concept

This series classifies the vocabulary into general vocabulary and specialized vocabulary. Based on the general vocabulary, it focuses on conceptual and behavioral words, not deviating from workplace situations, so as to control the vocabulary, work scenarios and content and means of communication, and build the semantic framework. The scientific integration of language classification and specialty classification is the key to the successful compilation of textbooks.

Textbook Objectives

Language Skill Objectives

For students at the elementary level, they are trained to be familiar with basic general vocabulary and common specialized vocabulary in the workplace, and be able to use short sentences for simple communication in life and at work. For those at the intermediate level, they are trained to understand simple conversations and speeches in the workplace, comprehend the main ideas, grasp the basic situations, and communicate with others in simple words on important topics at work. For those at the advanced level, they are trained to be able to understand general conversations and speeches in the workplace, grasp the main content and key information, use basic communication strategies to communicate with others and carry out the work, have a preliminary understanding of cultural factors related to communication activities, master the general communication-related cultural background knowledge, and overcome cultural barriers encountered during communication. The progression in level of communicative competence helps them to leap forward from routine etiquette, basic communication in life and at work at the elementary level, to simple information exchange of service processes at the intermediate level, and finally to complex information exchange and handling of special circumstances at the advanced level.

Vocational Skill Objectives

To meet job requirements at the elementary, intermediate and advanced levels, the professional positions that are most urgently needed overseas are selected. The positions corresponding to logistics management at the elementary, intermediate and advanced levels are logistics staff, logistics managers and logistics directors; the positions corresponding to automotive service engineering technology at the elementary, intermediate and advanced levels are automotive electromechanical maintenance staff, automotive service consultants and technical directors; the positions corresponding to e-commerce at the elementary, intermediate and advanced levels are electronic operation assistants, e-commerce operators and e-commerce customer service staff; the positions corresponding to mechatronics at the elementary, intermediate and advanced levels are mechanical and electrical operators, mechanical and electrical adjusters, and mechanical and electrical maintenance staff; the positions corresponding to computer networking technology at the elementary, intermediate and advanced levels are broadband operation and maintenance engineers, network operation and maintenance specialists, and network administrators; the positions corresponding to hotel management at the elementary, intermediate and advanced levels are lobby receptionists, lobby supervisors and lobby managers. Through 30 work scenarios/tasks set for each major, learners can fully grasp the general situations and basic procedures of the position after learning, and achieve the dual goals of language learning and professional operation.

Principles of Compilation

1. Language knowledge skills and professional knowledge skills go hand in hand to meet the demands of current popular and urgently needed job positions;

2. It makes progressive differentiation and comprehensive integration, breaking down, dividing and conquering difficult points;

3. Language knowledge and professional knowledge recur scientifically and efficiently, language skills and professional skills spiral upward, and the situational stage, semantic framework, and ontology input methods cooperate with each other;

4. Professional knowledge and skills are visualized, using a lot of pictures and videos;

5. It strengthens the practical skills in professional positions. This series of textbooks is equipped with videos of professional technical training, highlighting the practical skills for professional positions. It addresses the mismatch between the difficulty of language learning and that of mastering skills by supplementing with practical videos and practical training.

Characteristic Pursuit

Starting from the basic phonetic knowledge learning and job cognition at the elementary level, this series integrates "Chinese + Vocational Skills" into the working scene dialogues, breaking down the job into various tasks, solving lexical students' problems by means of picture cognition, solving the problem of the mismatch between students' mastery of Chinese vocabulary and professional skills by means of displaying videos, stressing the practicality of skills, and focusing on "learning by doing". Each unit has a "Practicing What You Have Learnt" module, which not only solves the problem of lexical cognition of this unit, but also takes "being able to comprehend", "being able to use" and "being able to imitate" as the learning objectives. We strive to use a large number of pictures and display supporting videos to build the textbooks into three-dimensional skills-based language teaching materials, so that learners can learn more independently.

Recommendations for Use

1. Each major of this series consists of three volumes at the elementary, intermediate, and advanced levels, with 10 units in each volume. For each unit, it is recommended to be completed in 8-10 class hours at the elementary level, 10-12 class hours at the intermediate level, and 12-14 class hours at the advanced level.

2. The notes and explanations in the textbooks focus on conciseness, practicality, and the training of listening and speaking skills. The grammar knowledge in the textbooks can be detailed and supplemented by teachers as the case may be.

3. "Unit Practical Training" module can be used as a classroom exercise after the texts and language points, preferably to be completed in two class hours. Teachers should guide students to complete the training tasks step by step. Students are not required to read and understand the training steps. It is important that teachers guide students to achieve the goal of mastering professional skills.

4. "Unit Summary" module summarizes the keywords and core content of the entire unit. Through listening and speaking exercises, this part can better help learners understand the core tasks of this unit.

5. Teachers should make full use of the exercises designed in the textbooks during class, and guide students to listen more and practice more, combine listening and speaking, and integrate learning with practice.

6. Teachers should guide students to proficiently read the texts aloud, asking them to recite the keywords, sentences and classroom expressions in each unit.

Acknowledgements

We are grateful to the Center for Language Education and Cooperation of the Ministry of Education for listing the New Silk Road "Chinese + Vocational Skills" series as a key research and development project, which adds motivation and a sense of responsibility to our textbook compilation. The Textbook Compilation Committee is responsible for the planning, design, compilation and coordination of the entire set of textbooks, and has held hundreds of seminars to conduct a comprehensive evaluation, discussion, examination and approval of text compilation, style arrangement, notes and explanations, exercise design, picture selection, and video production of each textbook. We are indebted to the members of the Compilation Committee and all compilers for their professional dedication, unwavering pursuit of perfection in the compilation, as well as their enthusiasm, hard work and wisdom. We are thankful to the experts in international Chinese language education and colleagues from all over the country who have kept a close eye on this series and contributed their valuable opinions.

Compilation Committee of New Silk Road "Chinese + Vocational Skills" Series

April 2023

gǎngwèi jièshào
岗位介绍
Introduction to Posts

wǎngluò gōngchéngshī
网 络 工 程 师
Network Engineer

wǎngyè shèjìshī
网 页 设 计 师
Web Designer

wǎngzhàn wéihùyuán
网站 维护员
Website Maintainer

jìsuànjī xìtǒng wéihùyuán
计算机系统维护员
Computer System Maintainer

shùjùkù guǎnlǐ yǔ wéihù gōngchéngshī
数据库管理与维护工 程 师
Database Management & Maintenance Engineer

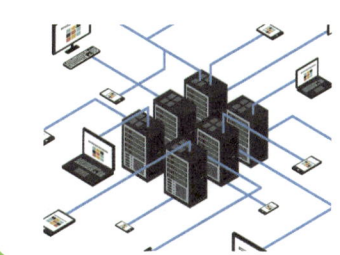

9

语法术语及缩略形式参照表
Abbreviations of Grammar Terms

Grammar Terms in Chinese	Grammar Terms in *Pinyin*	Grammar Terms in English	Abbreviations
名词	míngcí	noun	n.
专有名词	zhuānyǒu míngcí	proper noun	pn.
代词	dàicí	pronoun	pron.
数词	shùcí	numeral	num.
量词	liàngcí	measure word	m.
数量词	shùliàngcí	quantifier	q.
动词	dòngcí	verb	v.
助动词	zhùdòngcí	auxiliary	aux.
形容词	xíngróngcí	adjective	adj.
副词	fùcí	adverb	adv.
介词	jiècí	preposition	prep.
连词	liáncí	conjunction	conj.
助词	zhùcí	particle	part.
拟声词	nǐshēngcí	onomatopoeia	onom.
叹词	tàncí	interjection	int.
前缀	qiánzhuì	prefix	pref.
后缀	hòuzhuì	suffix	suf.
成语	chéngyǔ	idiom	idm.
短语	duǎnyǔ	phrase	phr.
主语	zhǔyǔ	subject	S
谓语	wèiyǔ	predicate	P
宾语	bīnyǔ	object	O
定语	dìngyǔ	attributive	Attrib
状语	zhuàngyǔ	adverbial	Adverb
补语	bǔyǔ	complement	C

CONTENTS 目录

第一单元 命令行的使用 Use of Command Line — 1

第一部分 课文 Texts — 2
- 一、热身 Warm-up — 2
- 二、课文 Texts — 4
- 三、视听说 Viewing, Listening and Speaking — 8
- 四、学以致用 Practicing What You Have Learnt — 9
- 五、小知识 Tips — 9

第二部分 汉字 Chinese Characters — 10
- 一、汉字知识 Knowledge about Chinese Characters — 10
  1. 汉字的笔画（1） Strokes of Chinese characters (1)
     一 丨 丿 丶
  2. 汉字的笔顺（1） Stroke orders of Chinese characters (1)
     先横后竖 Horizontal strokes before vertical strokes
     先撇后捺 Left-falling strokes before right-falling strokes
- 二、汉字认读与书写 The Recognition and Writing of Chinese Characters — 11

第三部分 日常用语 Daily Expressions — 11

第四部分 单元实训 Unit Practical Training — 11
- VRP 的使用 Use of VRP — 11

第五部分 单元小结 Unit Summary — 12

第二单元 通过 Console 口登录设备 Log in to the Device through the Console Port — 15

第一部分 课文 Texts — 16
- 一、热身 Warm-up — 16
- 二、课文 Texts — 17
- 三、视听说 Viewing, Listening and Speaking — 20
- 四、学以致用 Practicing What You Have Learnt — 21
- 五、小知识 Tips — 22

第二部分 汉字 Chinese Characters — 23
- 一、汉字知识 Knowledge about Chinese Characters — 23

I

  1. 汉字的笔画（2） Strokes of Chinese characters (2)

   丶 乛 乚 乙

  2. 汉字的笔顺（2） Stroke orders of Chinese characters (2)

   先上后下 Upper strokes before lower strokes

   先左后右 Left-side strokes before right-side strokes

 二、汉字认读与书写　The Recognition and Writing of Chinese Characters 24

第三部分　日常用语　**Daily Expressions** 24

第四部分　单元实训　**Unit Practical Training** 24

 通过 Console 口登录设备 Log in to the Device Through the Console Port 24

第五部分　单元小结　**Unit Summary** 25

第三单元　设备的基本配置　Basic Configuration of the Device 27

第一部分　课文　**Texts** 28

 一、热身　Warm-up 28

 二、课文　Texts 29

 三、视听说　Viewing, Listening and Speaking 33

 四、学以致用　Practicing What You Have Learnt 34

 五、小知识　Tips 35

第二部分　汉字　**Chinese Characters** 35

 一、汉字知识　Knowledge about Chinese Characters 35

  1. 汉字的笔画（3） Strokes of Chinese characters (3)

   ⺄ 亅 丿 乚

  2. 汉字的笔顺（3） Stroke orders of Chinese characters (3)

   先中间后两边 Strokes in the middle before those on both sides

   先外边后里边 Outside strokes before inside strokes

 二、汉字认读与书写　The Recognition and Writing of Chinese Characters 36

第三部分　日常用语　**Daily Expressions** 36

第四部分　单元实训　**Unit Practical Training** 37

 设备的基本配置 Basic Configuration of the Device 37

第五部分　单元小结　**Unit Summary** 38

第四单元　用户界面配置　User Interface Configuration 41

第一部分　课文　**Texts** 42

 一、热身　Warm-up 42

 二、课文　Texts 43

	三、视听说 Viewing, Listening and Speaking	46	
	四、学以致用 Practicing What You Have Learnt	47	
	五、小知识 Tips	48	
第二部分	汉字 **Chinese Characters**	49	
	一、汉字知识 Knowledge about Chinese Characters	49	
	1. 汉字的笔画（4） Strokes of Chinese characters (4)		
	2. 汉字的笔顺（4） Stroke orders of Chinese characters (4)		
	先外后里再封口 Outside strokes before inside strokes, and then sealing strokes		
	二、汉字认读与书写 The Recognition and Writing of Chinese Characters	49	
第三部分	日常用语 **Daily Expressions**	50	
第四部分	单元实训 **Unit Practical Training**	50	
	配置用户界面 Configuring User Interface	50	
第五部分	单元小结 **Unit Summary**	51	

第五单元　文件系统管理　File System Management　53

第一部分	课文 **Texts**	54
	一、热身 Warm-up	54
	二、课文 Texts	56
	三、视听说 Viewing, Listening and Speaking	59
	四、学以致用 Practicing What You Have Learnt	60
	五、小知识 Tips	61
第二部分	汉字 **Chinese Characters**	62
	一、汉字知识 Knowledge about Chinese Characters	62
	1. 汉字的笔画（5） Strokes of Chinese characters (5)	
	2. 汉字的结构（1） Structures of Chinese characters (1)	
	独体结构 Independent structure	
	二、汉字认读与书写 The Recognition and Writing of Chinese Characters	63
第三部分	日常用语 **Daily Expressions**	63
第四部分	单元实训 **Unit Practical Training**	63
	目录和文件命令 Directory and File Commands	63
第五部分	单元小结 **Unit Summary**	65

第六单元　配置文件管理　Configuration File Management　67

第一部分　课文　Texts　68
- 一、热身　Warm-up　68
- 二、课文　Texts　71
- 三、视听说　Viewing, Listening and Speaking　74
- 四、学以致用　Practicing What You Have Learnt　75
- 五、小知识　Tips　75

第二部分　汉字　Chinese Characters　76
- 一、汉字知识　Knowledge about Chinese Characters　76
    1. 汉字的笔画（6）　Strokes of Chinese characters (6)
        乛 ㇈
    2. 汉字的结构（2）　Structures of Chinese characters (2)
        品字形结构　品-shaped structure
- 二、汉字认读与书写　The Recognition and Writing of Chinese Characters　77

第三部分　日常用语　Daily Expressions　77
第四部分　单元实训　Unit Practical Training　77
配置文件的操作　Operations on Configuration File　78
第五部分　单元小结　Unit Summary　79

第七单元　虚拟局域网　Virtual Local Area Network　81

第一部分　课文　Texts　82
- 一、热身　Warm-up　82
- 二、课文　Texts　85
- 三、视听说　Viewing, Listening and Speaking　88
- 四、学以致用　Practicing What You Have Learnt　89
- 五、小知识　Tips　90

第二部分　汉字　Chinese Characters　91
- 一、汉字知识　Knowledge about Chinese Characters　91
    1. 汉字的笔画（7）　Strokes of Chinese characters (7)
        ㇉ ㇋
    2. 汉字的结构（3）　Structures of Chinese characters (3)
        上下结构　Top-bottom structure
        上中下结构　Top-middle-bottom structure
- 二、汉字认读与书写　The Recognition and Writing of Chinese Characters　91

第三部分　日常用语　Daily Expressions　92

IV

第四部分　单元实训　**Unit Practical Training** 　92
　　VLAN 的划分 Division of VLAN 　92
第五部分　单元小结　**Unit Summary** 　93

第八单元　地址与子网掩码　IP Address and Subnet Mask　95

第一部分　课文　**Texts**　96
　　一、热身　Warm-up　96
　　二、课文　Texts　98
　　三、视听说　Viewing, Listening and Speaking　101
　　四、学以致用　Practicing What You Have Learnt　102
　　五、小知识　Tips　103

第二部分　汉字　**Chinese Characters**　104
　　一、汉字知识　Knowledge about Chinese Characters　104
　　　　1. 汉字的笔画（8）　Strokes of Chinese characters (8)
　　　　2. 汉字的结构（4）　Structures of Chinese characters (4)
　　　　　左右结构 Left-right structure
　　　　　左中右结构 Left-middle-right structure
　　二、汉字认读与书写　The Recognition and Writing of Chinese Characters　104

第三部分　日常用语　**Daily Expressions**　105

第四部分　单元实训　**Unit Practical Training**　105
　　配置 IP 地址并验证连通性 Configuring IP Address and Verifying the Connectivity　105

第五部分　单元小结　**Unit Summary**　106

第九单元　用路由器组建网络　Constructing a Network with Routers　109

第一部分　课文　**Texts**　110
　　一、热身　Warm-up　110
　　二、课文　Texts　113
　　三、视听说　Viewing, Listening and Speaking　115
　　四、学以致用　Practicing What You Have Learnt　116
　　五、小知识　Tips　117

第二部分　汉字　**Chinese Characters**　117
　　一、汉字知识　Knowledge about Chinese Characters　117
　　　　1. 汉字的笔画（9）　Strokes of Chinese characters (9)

V

2. 汉字的结构（5） Structures of Chinese characters (5)
      全包围结构 Fully-enclosed structure
      半包围结构 Semi-enclosed structure
    二、汉字认读与书写　The Recognition and Writing of Chinese Characters　118
 第三部分　日常用语　**Daily Expressions**　118
 第四部分　单元实训　**Unit Practical Training**　119
    配置静态路由 Configuring Static Routing　119
 第五部分　单元小结　**Unit Summary**　120

第十单元　地址管理　IP Address Management　121

 第一部分　课文　**Texts**　122
    一、热身　Warm-up　122
    二、课文　Texts　125
    三、视听说　Viewing, Listening and Speaking　128
    四、学以致用　Practicing What You Have Learnt　129
    五、小知识　Tips　130
 第二部分　汉字　**Chinese Characters**　131
    一、汉字知识　Knowledge about Chinese Characters　131
      1. 汉字的笔画（总表） Strokes of Chinese characters (general table)
      2. 汉字的笔顺（总表） Stroke orders of Chinese characters (general table)
      3. 汉字的结构（总表） Structures of Chinese characters (general table)
    二、汉字认读与书写　The Recognition and Writing of Chinese Characters　132
 第三部分　日常用语　**Daily Expressions**　132
 第四部分　单元实训　**Unit Practical Training**　132
    DHCP 的配置 Configuration of DHCP　133
 第五部分　单元小结　**Unit Summary**　134

附录　Appendix　136

 词语总表　Vocabulary　136
 视频脚本　Video Scripts　145
 参考答案　Reference Answers　152

VI

1

Mìnglìngháng de shǐyòng
命令行的使用
Use of Command Line

VRP mìnglìng de jiǎndān shǐyòng
VRP 命令的 简单 使用
Simple Use of VRP Commands

```
The device is running!

<Huawei>
<Huawei>
```
qǐdòng shèbèi, bìng jìnrù mìnglìngháng jièmiàn
启动 设备，并 进入 命令行 界面
start the device, and enter the command line interface

```
The device is running!

<Huawei>
<Huawei>system-view
Enter system view, return user view with
[Huawei]
```
shūrù "system-view" mìnglìng, jìnrù xìtǒng shìtú
输入 "system-view" 命令，进入系统视图
enter the "system-view" command to enter the system view

```
<Huawei>system-view
Enter system view, return user view with Ctrl+Z.
[Huawei]interface GigabitEthernet 0/0/1
[Huawei-GigabitEthernet0/0/1]
```
shūrù "interface" mìnglìng, jìnrù jiēkǒu shìtú
输入 "interface" 命令，进入接口视图
enter the "interface" command to enter the interface view

```
<Huawei>system-view
Enter system view, return user view with Ctrl+Z.
[Huawei]interface GigabitEthernet 0/0/1
[Huawei-GigabitEthernet0/0/1]quit
[Huawei]
```
zài shūrù "quit" mìnglìng, cóng dāngqián shìtú tuìchū zhì shàng yì céng shìtú
再输入 "quit" 命令，从 当前 视图退出至 上 一 层 视图
enter the "quit" command to quit from the current view and return to the previous view

```
<Huawei>?
User view commands:
  arp-ping           ARP-ping
  autosave           <Group> autosave command group
  backup             Backup information
  cd                 Change current directory
  clear              <Group> clear command group
  clock              Specify the system clock
  cls                Clear screen
  compare            Compare configuration file
  copy               Copy from one file to another
  debugging          <Group> debugging command group
  delete             Delete a file
  dialer             Dialer
  dir                List files on a filesystem
  display            Display information
  factory-configuration  Factory configuration
  fixdisk            Try to restory disk
  format             Format file system
  free               Release a user terminal interface
  ftp                Establish an FTP connection
  help               Description of the interactive he
  hwtacacs-user      HWTACACS user
  license            <Group> license command group
  lldp               Link Layer Discovery Protocol
 ---- More ----
```
shūrù "?" mìnglìng, huòdé zàixiàn bāngzhù
输入 "?" 命令，获得 在线 帮助
enter the "?" command to get online help

1

> **题解　Introduction**
>
> 1. 学习内容：VRP 命令行的概念、命令级别、权限和使用方法。
>   Learning content: The concept, command level, access permission and usage of VRP command line.
> 2. 知识目标：掌握 VRP 命令行使用过程中的核心词语，学习汉字的笔画 "一、丨、丿、丶" 和笔顺 "先横后竖、先撇后捺"，学写相关汉字。
>   Knowledge objectives: To master the core vocabulary used in the process of using VRP command line, learn the strokes "一, 丨, 丿, 丶" and the stroke order "horizontal strokes before vertical strokes, left-falling strokes before right-falling strokes" of Chinese characters, and write the related characters.
> 3. 技能目标：通过对 VRP 命令行概念、命令级别、权限等的学习，学会 VRP 的简单使用。
>   Skill objective: To master the simple use of VRP through learning the concept, command level and access permission of VRP command line.

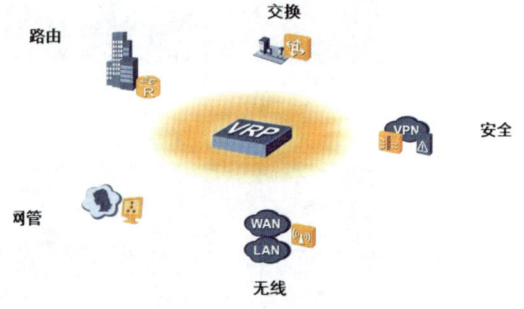

第一部分　Part 1

课文　Texts

一、热身　rèshēn　Warm-up

1. 下面所给的是 VRP 相关图示，请给词语选择对应的图示。
   The following are the pictures related to VRP. Please choose the corresponding pictures for the words and phrases.

A.
- 多进程
- 组件化设计
- 支持多CPU、多框

B.

操作	命令
设置路由器名	sysname

C.

D.

操作	命令
从用户视图进入系统视图	system-view
从系统视图返回到用户视图	quit
从任意的非用户视图返回到用户视图	return

命令行的使用
Use of Command Line

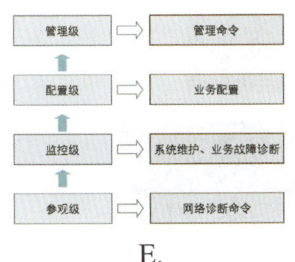

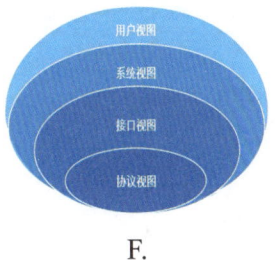

E. F.

      VRP　píngtái
❶ VRP 平台_____
    VRP platform

      VRP　cāozuò　xìtǒng　mìnglìngháng shìtú
❷ VRP 操作系统 命令行 视图 _____
    VRP operating system command line view

      VRP8　bǎnběn tèxìng
❸ VRP8 版本特性_____
    features of VRP8 version

      mìnglìng　de　jíbié
❹ 命令 的级别_____
    level of commands

      jìnrù　hé tuìchū xìtǒng　shìtú
❺ 进入和退出系统视图_____
    entering and quiting the system view

      pèizhì　lùyóuqì　míngchēng
❻ 配置路由器 名称 _____
    configuring the router

2. 观看介绍 VRP 命令的简单使用的视频，将这些命令、界面或视图与对应图片连线。
   Watch the video introducing the simple use of VRP commands, and match the commands, interfaces or views with the corresponding pictures.

3

① zàixiàn bāngzhù mìnglìng
在线 帮助 命令
online help command

② mìnglìngháng jièmiàn
命令行 界面
command line interface

③ jìnrù xìtǒng shìtú
进入 系统 视图
enter the system view

④ tuìchū mìnglìngháng shìtú
退出 命令行 视图
quit the command line view

⑤ jiēkǒu shìtú
接口视图
interface view

A.
B.
C.
D.
E.

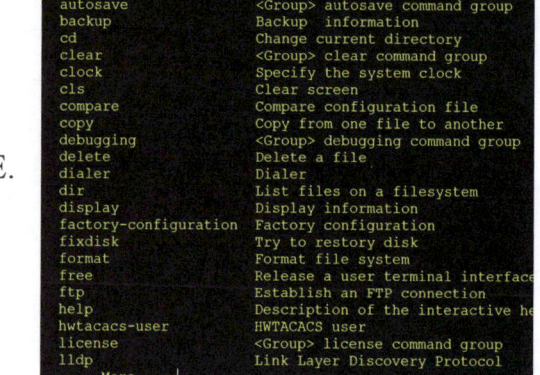

二、课文 kèwén Texts

 01-01

túdì: Shīfu, qǐngwèn shénme shì VRP?
徒弟：师傅，请问 什么是 VRP？

shīfu: VRP shì Zhōngguó Huáwéi Gōngsī shùjù tōngxìn chǎnpǐn de tōngyòng wǎngluò cāozuò
师傅：VRP 是 中国 华为 公司数据通信产品 的 通用 网络 操作

xìtǒng.
系统。

1 Use of Command Line
命令行的使用

túdì:　　VRP　yǒu shénme yōudiǎn ma?
徒弟：VRP 有 什么 优点 吗？

shīfu:　　VRP　jùyǒu gāo kěkàoxìng、 gāo xìngnéng、 gāo kěkuòzhǎnxìng děng yōudiǎn.
师傅：VRP 具有 高可靠性、 高 性能、 高 可扩展性 等 优点。

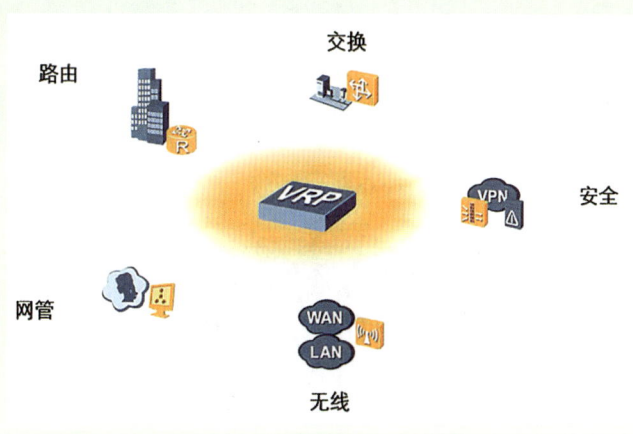

译文 yìwén Text in English

Apprentice: Master, what is the VRP?
Master: The VRP is a general-purpose network operating system for data communication products of Huawei, a Chinese company.
Apprentice: What are the advantages of the VRP?
Master: The VRP has the advantages of high reliability, high performance and extensibility, etc.

普通词语 pǔtōng cíyǔ General Vocabulary　🎧 01-02

1.	中国	Zhōngguó	pn.	China
2.	华为公司	Huáwéi Gōngsī	pn.	Huawei Company
3.	产品	chǎnpǐn	n.	product
4.	通用	tōngyòng	adj.	all-purpose, universal
5.	网络	wǎngluò	n.	network
6.	优点	yōudiǎn	n.	advantage

专业词语 zhuānyè cíyǔ Specialized Vocabulary　🎧 01-03

1.	VRP			Versatile Routing Platform
2.	数据	shùjù	n.	data
3.	通信	tōngxìn	n.	communication

5

4.	系统	xìtǒng	n.	system
5.	高	gāo	adj.	high
6.	可靠性	kěkàoxìng	n.	reliability
7.	性能	xìngnéng	n.	performance
8.	可扩展性	kěkuòzhǎnxìng	n.	extensibility

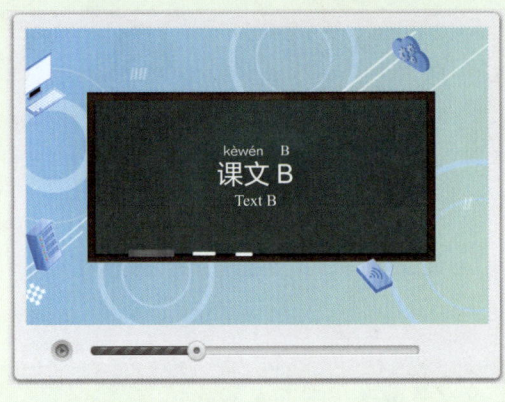

徒弟：师傅，VRP 命令行的作用是什么？

师傅：VRP 命令行用来完成华为网络设备功能的配置和业务的部署。

徒弟：一条 VRP 命令行的结构是怎样的呢？

师傅：一条 VRP 命令行由关键字和参数组成。

徒弟：VRP 命令有几个级别？

师傅：VRP 命令级别分为 0～3 级。

1 Use of Command Line
命令行的使用

VRP mìnglìngháng jiégòu
VRP 命令行结构
structure of VRP command line

mìnglìng jíbié
命令级别
command level

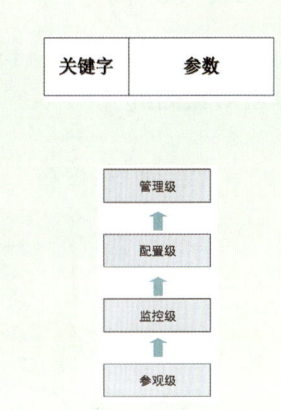

译文 yìwén Text in English

Apprentice: Master, what is the function of the VRP command line?
Master: The VRP command line is used to complete the configuration of functions of Huawei network equipment and the deployment of businesses.
Apprentice: What is the structure of a VRP command line?
Master: A VRP command line consists of keywords and parameters.
Apprentice: How many levels does the VRP command have?
Master: The VRP command can be divided into levels 0-3.

普通词语 pǔtōng cíyǔ General Vocabulary 🎧 01-05

1.	作用	zuòyòng	n.	function
2.	完成	wán//chéng	v.	complete
3.	功能	gōngnéng	n.	function
4.	业务	yèwù	n.	business
5.	部署	bùshǔ	v.	deploy
6.	怎样	zěnyàng	pron.	how
7.	个	gè	m.	*a measure word*
8.	级别	jíbié	n.	level
9.	分为	fēnwéi	phr.	be divided into

专业词语 zhuānyè cíyǔ Specialized Vocabulary 🎧 01-06

1.	命令行	mìnglìngháng	phr.	command line
2.	关键字	guānjiànzì	phr.	keyword
	关键	guānjiàn	n.	key
	字	zì	n.	word, character

7

三、视听说 shì-tīng-shuō Viewing, Listening and Speaking

1. 观看介绍 VRP 命令级别的视频，将命令级别与它们的作用连线。
Watch the video introducing VRP command levels, and match the command levels with their functions.

① 0 jí: cānguānjí mìnglìng
 0 级：参观级命令
 Level 0: visit-level command

A. chákàn wǎngluò zhuàngtài hé shèbèi jīběn xìnxī
 查看网络状态和设备基本信息
 to view the network status and basic device information

② 1 jí: jiānkòngjí mìnglìng
 1 级：监控级命令
 Level 1: monitoring-level command

B. cèshì wǎngluò shìfǒu liántōng
 测试网络是否连通
 to test whether the network is connected

③ 2 jí: pèizhìjí mìnglìng
 2 级：配置级命令
 Level 2: configuration-level command

C. shàngchuán huòzhě xiàzài pèizhì wénjiàn
 上传或者下载配置文件
 to upload or download configuration files

④ 3 jí: guǎnlǐjí mìnglìng
 3 级：管理级命令
 Level 3: management-level command

D. yèwù pèizhì
 业务配置
 to configure businesses

2. 说一说 Let's talk.

说一说 VRP 四个命令级别的作用分别是什么。
Talk about the functions of the four levels of VRP commands respectively.

四、学以致用 xuéyǐzhìyòng Practicing What You Have Learnt

观看视频，找出 VRP 命令级别在实际的运用中对应的用户级别。
Watch the video, and find out the user levels corresponding to the VRP command levels in practical applications.

A. VRP 命令级别 0、1、2、3
VRP command levels 0, 1, 2 and 3

B. VRP 命令级别 0、1
VRP command levels 0 and 1

C. VRP 命令级别 0、1、2
VRP command levels 0, 1 and 2

D. VRP 命令级别 0
VRP command level 0

❶ VRP 用户级别 0＿＿＿＿＿＿＿
VRP user level 0

❷ VRP 用户级别 1＿＿＿＿＿＿＿
VRP user level 1

❸ VRP 用户级别 2＿＿＿＿＿＿＿
VRP user level 2

❹ VRP 用户级别 3～15＿＿＿＿＿＿＿
VRP user levels 3-15

五、小知识 xiǎo zhīshi Tips

VRP 平台的作用 VRP píngtái de zuòyòng

VRP 平台以 TCP/IP 协议栈为核心，实现了数据链路层、网络层和应用层的多种协议，在操作系统中集成了多种数据通信要件，并以 IP 转发引擎技术为基础，为网络设备提供了出色的数据转发能力。

Functions of the VRP Platform

Taking TCP/IP protocol stack as the core, the VRP platform realizes a variety of protocols at data link layer, network layer and application layer, integrates a variety of data communication elements in the operating system, and provides excellent data forwarding capability for network devices based on IP forwarding engine technology.

补充专业词语 bǔchōng zhuānyè cíyǔ Supplementary Specialized Vocabulary 🎧 01-07

1.	版本特性	bǎnběn tèxìng	phr.	version property
2.	系统视图	xìtǒng shìtú	phr.	system view
	视图	shìtú	n.	view
3.	接口视图	jiēkǒu shìtú	phr.	interface view
4.	用户级别	yònghù jíbié	phr.	user level
	用户	yònghù	n.	user

第二部分 Part 2 汉字 Chinese Characters

一、汉字知识 Hànzì zhīshi Knowledge about Chinese Characters

1. 汉字的笔画（1） Strokes of Chinese characters (1)

笔画 Strokes	名称 Names	例字 Examples
一	横 héng	二
丨	竖 shù	十
丿	撇 piě	人
丶	捺 nà	八

2. 汉字的笔顺（1） Stroke orders of Chinese characters (1)

规则 Rules	例字 Examples	笔顺 Stroke orders
先横后竖 Horizontal strokes before vertical strokes	十	一 十
先撇后捺 Left-falling strokes before right-falling strokes	人 八	丿 人 丿 八

二、汉字认读与书写 Hànzì rèndú yǔ shūxiě The Recognition and Writing of Chinese Characters

认读下列汉字构成的词语，并试着写汉字。
Read the words composed of the following Chinese characters, and try to write them.

版本特性　　操作系统　　关键字　　级别

版				本				特				性			
操				作				系				统			
关				键				字				级			
别															

第三部分　Part 3   日常用语 Daily Expressions

① 劳驾，帮我叫辆出租车。Láojià, bāng wǒ jiào liàng chūzūchē. Excuse me, please get me a taxi.
② 明天见。Míngtiān jiàn. See you tomorrow!
③ 不见不散。Bú jiàn bú sàn. Be there or be square!

第四部分　Part 4   单元实训 Unit Practical Training

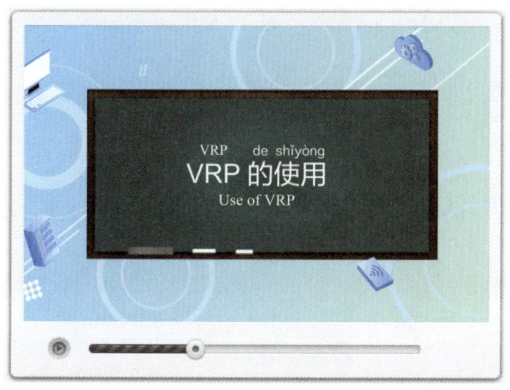

VRP de shǐyòng
VRP 的使用 Use of VRP

实训目的 Training purpose
学会 VRP 的简单使用。
To learn the simple use of VRP.

实训组织 Training organization

每组 3～5 人，选出一个组长。

Students work in groups of 3-5. Each group chooses a group leader.

实训内容 Training content

VRP 的使用。

Use of VRP.

实训步骤 Training steps

❶ 通过跟读、图片展示及小组比赛等方式复习巩固 VRP 使用命令。

Review and consolidate VRP commands through listening and repeating, picture presentation, group competition and other methods.

❷ 进入系统视图界面。

Enter the system view interface.

❸ 修改路由器名称为 R1。

Change the router name to R1.

❹ 路由器 R1 配置显示相关信息等。

Router R1 configuration displays relevant information, etc.

❺ 实训结束，总结评价。

The teacher makes a summary and an evaluation, and ends the training.

第五部分　Part 5

单元小结　Unit Summary

普通词语　General Vocabulary

cíyǔ 词语 Vocabulary

1.	中国	Zhōngguó	pn.	China
2.	华为公司	Huáwéi Gōngsī	pn.	Huawei Company
3.	产品	chǎnpǐn	n.	product
4.	通用	tōngyòng	adj.	all-purpose, universal
5.	网络	wǎngluò	n.	network
6.	优点	yōudiǎn	n.	advantage
7.	作用	zuòyòng	n.	function
8.	完成	wán//chéng	v.	complete
9.	功能	gōngnéng	n.	function
10.	业务	yèwù	n.	business
11.	部署	bùshǔ	v.	deploy

词语 Vocabulary (cíyǔ)

12.	怎样	zěnyàng	pron.	how
13.	个	gè	m.	*a measure word*
14.	级别	jíbié	n.	level
15.	分为	fēnwéi	phr.	be divided into

专业词语 Specialized Vocabulary

1.	VRP			Versatile Routing Platform
2.	数据	shùjù	n.	data
3.	通信	tōngxìn	n.	communication
4.	系统	xìtǒng	n.	system
5.	高	gāo	adj.	high
6.	可靠性	kěkàoxìng	n.	reliability
7.	性能	xìngnéng	n.	performance
8.	可扩展性	kěkuòzhǎnxìng	n.	extensibility
9.	命令行	mìnglìngháng	phr.	command line
10.	关键字	guānjiànzì	phr.	keyword
	关键	guānjiàn	n.	key
	字	zì	n.	word, character

补充专业词语 Supplementary Specialized Vocabulary

1.	版本特性	bǎnběn tèxìng	phr.	version property
2.	系统视图	xìtǒng shìtú	phr.	system view
	视图	shìtú	n.	view
3.	接口视图	jiēkǒu shìtú	phr.	interface view
4.	用户级别	yònghù jíbié	phr.	user level
	用户	yònghù	n.	user

句子 Sentences (jùzi)

1. VRP是中国华为公司数据通信产品的通用网络操作系统。
2. VRP具有高可靠性、高性能、高可扩展性等优点。
3. VRP命令行用来完成华为网络设备功能的配置和业务的部署。
4. 一条VRP命令行由关键字和参数组成。
5. VRP命令级别分为0～3级。

2

Tōngguò Console kǒu dēnglù shèbèi
通过 Console 口登录设备
Log in to the Device through the Console Port

tōngguò Console kǒu dēnglù shèbèi bìng pèizhì tōngxìn ruǎnjiàn de bùzhòu
通过 Console 口 登录 设备 并 配置 通信 软件 的 步骤
Steps to Log in to the Device through the Console Port and Configure the Communication Software

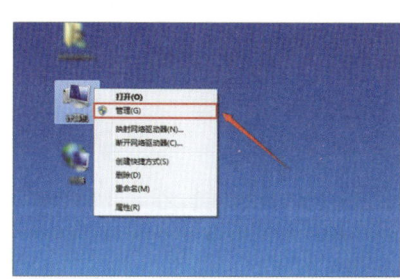

shǔbiāo yòujiàn diǎnjī "jìsuànjī", xuǎnzé "guǎnlǐ"
鼠标 右键 点击 "计算机", 选择 "管理"
right-click "Computer" and select "Manage"

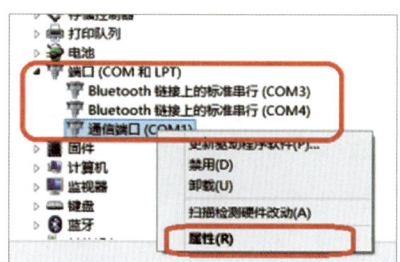

chákàn COM kǒu biānhào
查看 COM 口 编号
check the number of the COM port

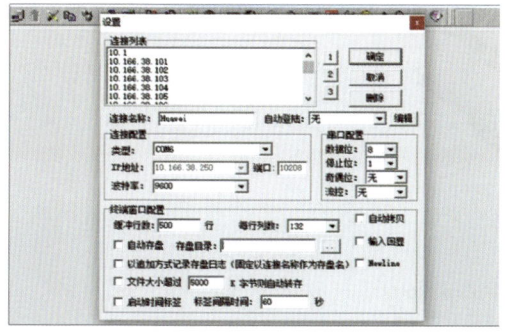

shèzhì "liánjiē míngchēng", "lèixíng" zhōng xuǎnzé duìyìng
设置 "连接 名称", "类型" 中 选择 对应
de COM biānhào, diǎnjī "quèdìng"
的 COM 编号, 点击 "确定"
set "Connection Name", select the corresponding COM number in "Type", and click "OK"

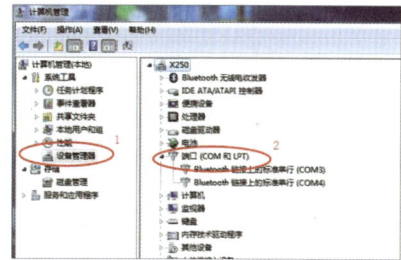

shǔbiāo zuǒjiàn diǎnjī "shèbèi guǎnlǐqì", zài yòucè
鼠标 左键 点击 "设备管理器", 在 右侧
chuāngkǒu xuǎnzé "duānkǒu"
窗口 选择 "端口"
left-click "Device Manager" and select "Port" in the right window

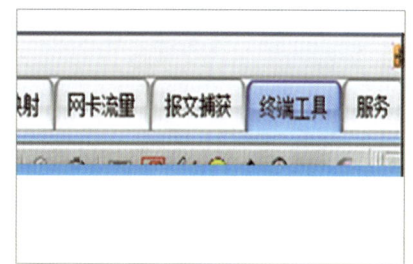

dǎkāi tōngxìn ruǎnjiàn, diǎnjī "zhōngduān gōngjù"
打开 通信 软件, 点击 "终端 工具"
biāoqiānlán, diǎnjī "xīn jiàn liánjiē"
标签栏, 点击 "新 建 连接"
open the communication software, click the "Terminal Tool" tab bar, and click "New Connection"

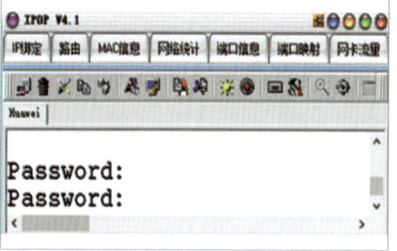

jiǎnchá liánjiē shìfǒu chénggōng
检查 连接 是否 成功
check whether it is successfully connected

15

题解 Introduction

1. 学习内容：Console 端口及设备的常用图标含义，通过 Console 口登录并配置设备的流程。
   Learning content: The meaning of the common icons of the Console port and the devices, and the process of logging in and configuring devices through the Console port.

2. 知识目标：掌握通过 Console 口登录并配置设备的流程中关键步骤的核心词语，学习汉字的笔画"、、フ、レ、ノ"和笔顺"先上后下，先左后右"，学写相关汉字。
   Knowledge objectives: To master the core vocabulary used in the key steps in the process of logging in and configuring devices through the Console port, learn the strokes "、, フ, レ, ノ" and the stroke order "upper strokes before lower strokes, left-side strokes before right-side strokes" of Chinese characters, and write the related characters.

3. 技能目标：学会操作通过 Console 口登录并配置设备。
   Skill objective: To learn to log in and configure devices through the Console port.

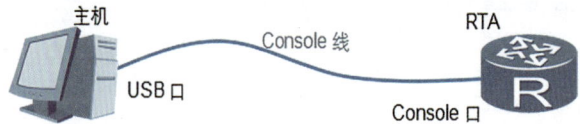

第一部分 Part 1

课文 Texts

一、热身 rèshēn Warm-up

1. 下图是一根 Console 电缆，请将所给词语填入相应位置。
   The picture below shows a Console cable. Please fill in the corresponding positions with the given words and phrases.

A. USB kǒu
   USB 口
   USB port

B. RJ45 jiēkǒu
   RJ45 接口
   RJ45 interface

通过 Console 口登录设备 **2**
Log in to the Device through the Console Port

2. 观看介绍用 Console 线连接电脑与设备的视频，将连接的步骤填入对应位置。
   Watch the video introducing the use of the Console cable to connect the computer and the device, and fill in the corresponding positions with the connecting steps.

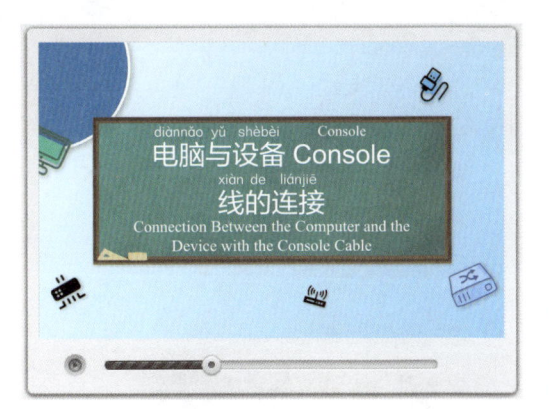

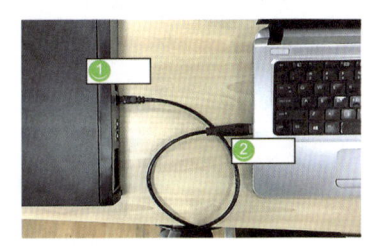

A. 　　Jiāng xiànlǎn USB kǒu chārù diànnǎo USB jiēkǒu.
　　将 线缆 USB 口插入电脑 USB 接口。
   Insert the USB port of the cable into the USB interface of the computer.

B. 　　Jiāng xiànlǎn RJ45 jiēkǒu chārù shèbèi Console duānkǒu.
　　将 线缆 RJ45 接口插入设备 Console 端口。
   Insert the RJ45 interface of the cable into the Console port of the device.

二、课文　kèwén　Texts

A 02-01

徒弟：　túdì: Shénme shì tōngguò console kǒu dēnglù shèbèi?
　　　什么是通过 Console 口登录设备？

17

师傅：就是通过网络设备的 Console 口实现设备与电脑的通信。

徒弟：为什么这样登录设备？

师傅：因为设备在初始状态下没有IP地址，设备端只能通过 Console 口通信。

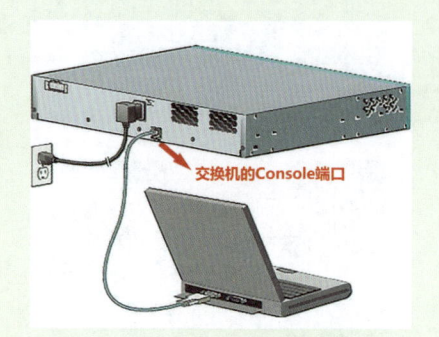

译文 yìwén Text in English

Apprentice: What is logging in to the device through the Console port?

Master: It is to realize the communication between the device and the computer through the Console port of the network device.

Apprentice: Why do we log in to the device in this way?

Master: Because the device has no IP address in its initial state, it can only communicate through the Console port.

普通词语 pǔtōng cíyǔ General Vocabulary 🎧 02-02

1.	通过	tōngguò	prep.	through
2.	实现	shíxiàn	v.	realize
3.	与	yǔ	conj.	and
4.	为什么	wèi shénme	phr.	why
5.	这样	zhèyàng	pron.	such
6.	因为	yīnwèi	conj.	because
7.	初始	chūshǐ	n.	inception, initial stage
8.	状态	zhuàngtài	n.	state
9.	下	xià	n.	being in
10.	没有	méiyǒu	v.	not have
11.	只	zhǐ	adv.	only

通过 Console 口登录设备
Log in to the Device through the Console Port

专业词语 zhuānyè cíyǔ Specialized Vocabulary 🎧 02-03

1.	Console 口	Console kǒu	phr.	Console port
	口	kǒu	n.	port
2.	设备端	shèbèiduān	phr.	on-device, device side

B 🎧 02-04

课文 B
Text B

徒弟: Shīfu, rúhé liánjiē wǎngluò shèbèi yǔ diànnǎo?
师傅，如何连接网络设备与电脑？

师傅: Xūyào yòng yì gēn Console xiànlǎn lái liánjiē, yì duān chā zài diànnǎo cè de USB
需要用一根 Console 线缆来连接，一端插在电脑侧的 USB
kǒu shang, lìng yì duān chā zài shèbèi de Console kǒu shang.
口上，另一端插在设备的 Console 口上。

徒弟: Suǒyǒu diànnǎo dōu yǒu USB kǒu ma?
所有电脑都有 USB 口吗？

师傅: Shìde. USB kǒu shì suǒyǒu diànnǎo de bìbèi jiēkǒu.
是的。USB 口是所有电脑的必备接口。

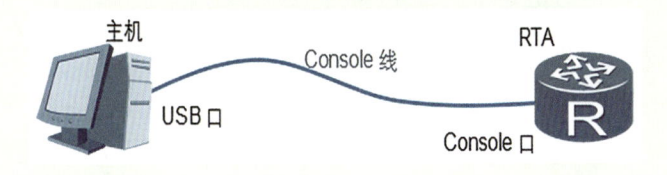

译文 yìwén Text in English

Apprentice: Master, how to connect the network device to the computer?

Master: You need a Console cable to make the connection, with one end of the cable plugged into the USB port on the computer side, and the other end plugged into the Console port on the device.

Apprentice: Do all computers have USB ports?

Master: Yes. USB port is a necessary interface for all computers.

普通词语 pǔtōng cíyǔ General Vocabulary 🎧 02-05

1.	用	yòng	v.	use
2.	根	gēn	m.	a measure word for something long and thin
3.	一端	yì duān	phr.	one end
4.	插	chā	v.	plug
5.	侧	cè	n.	side
6.	上	shang	n.	upside
7.	另	lìng	pron.	other
8.	所有	suǒyǒu	adj.	all
9.	都	dōu	adv.	all, both
10.	必备	bìbèi	v.	be necessary
11.	接口	jiēkǒu	n.	interface

专业词语 zhuānyè cíyǔ Specialized Vocabulary 🎧 02-06

USB 口	USB kǒu	phr.	USB port

三、视听说 shì-tīng-shuō Viewing, Listening and Speaking

1. 观看介绍通过 Console 口登录设备并配置通信软件的视频，对以下步骤进行排序。
Watch the video that introduces logging in to the device through the Console port and configuring the communication software, and arrange the following steps in order.

通过 Console 口登录设备
并配置通信软件的步骤
Steps of Logging in to the Device through the Console
Port and Configuring the Communication Software

A. 鼠标 右键点击 "计算机"，选择 "管理"。
Shǔbiāo yòujiàn diǎnjī "jìsuànjī", xuǎnzé "guǎnlǐ".
Right-click "Computer" and select "Manage".

B. 鼠标 左键点击 "设备管理器"，在右侧 窗口 选择 "端 口"。
Shǔbiāo zuǒjiàn diǎnjī "shèbèi guǎnlǐqì", zài yòucè chuāngkǒu xuǎnzé "duānkǒu".
Left-click "Device Manager" and select "Port" in the right window.

通过 Console 口登录设备
Log in to the Device through the Console Port

C. 查看 COM 口编号。
   Cházàn COM kǒu biānhào.
   Check the number of the COM port.

D. 打开通信软件，点击"终端工具"标签栏，点击"新建连接"。
   Dǎkāi tōngxìn ruǎnjiàn, diǎnjī "zhōngduān gōngjù" biāoqiānlán, diǎnjī "xīn jiàn liánjiē".
   Open the communication software, click the "Terminal Tool" tab bar, and then click "New Connection".

E. 设置"连接名称"，"类型"中选择对应的 COM 编号，点击"确定"。
   Shèzhì "liánjiē míngchēng", "lèixíng" zhōng xuǎnzé duìyìng de COM biānhào, diǎnjī "quèdìng".
   Set "Connection Name", select the corresponding COM number in "Type", and click "OK".

F. 检查连接是否成功。
   Jiǎnchá liánjiē shìfǒu chénggōng.
   Check whether it is successfully connected.

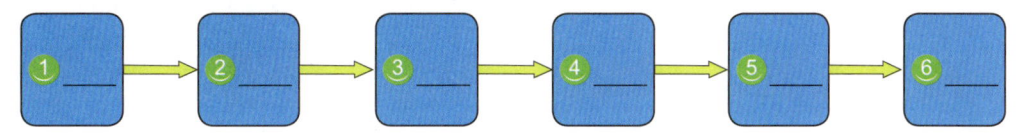

① ___ → ② ___ → ③ ___ → ④ ___ → ⑤ ___ → ⑥ ___

2. 说一说 Let's talk.

说一说通过 Console 口登录设备并配置通信软件的步骤。
Talk about the steps of logging in to the device through the Console port and configuring the communication software.

四、学以致用 xuéyǐzhìyòng Practicing What You Have Learnt

观看介绍通过 Console 口连接设备的过程的视频，将这些操作与匹配的图标连线。
Watch the video introducing the process of connecting the device through the Console port, and match the corresponding icons with these operations.

通过 Console 口
tōngguò Console kǒu
连接设备的过程
liánjiē shèbèi de guòchéng
Process of Connecting the Device through the Console Port

Yòng chuànkǒuxiàn liánjiē diànnǎo yǔ shèbèi.
❶ 用 串口线 连接电脑与设备。
Connect the computer and the device with a serial line.

A.

Dǎkāi diànnǎo de "shèbèi guǎnlǐqì".
❷ 打开电脑的"设备管理器"。
Open "Device Manager" of the computer.

B.

Zhǎodào diànnǎo shang de USB chuànxíngduānkǒu biānhào.
❸ 找到电脑 上的USB 串行 端口编号。
Find the number of the USB serial port on the computer.

C.

Dǎkāi IPOP ruǎnjiàn, diǎnjī "zhōngduān gōngjù"
❹ 打开IPOP 软件,点击"终端 工具"
biāoqiān.
标 签。
Open the IPOP software, and click "Terminal Tool" tab.

D.

Shèzhì liánjiē cānshù.
❺ 设置连接参数。
Set connection parameters.

E.

Shèbèi liánjiē chénggōng.
❻ 设备连接 成功。
The device is connected successfully.

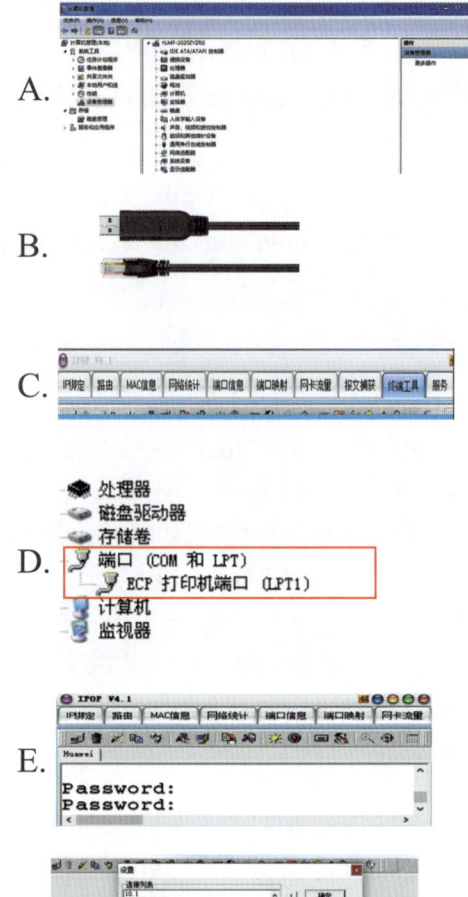

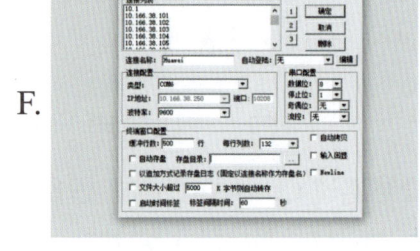

F.

五、小知识　xiǎo zhīshi　Tips

USB kǒu dēnglù fāngshì
USB 口 登录方式

Yǐqián, diànnǎoduān de console kǒu shì 9 zhēn D xíng kǒu. Xiànzài, bǐjìběn diàn-
以前, 电脑端 的 Console 口是9针D 型 口。现在, 笔记本电

nǎo shang yìbān bú pèizhì D xíng chākǒu, shènzhì hěn duō táishì diànnǎo shang yě bú pèizhì D xíng kǒu.
脑 上 一般 不配置D型 插口, 甚至 很 多台式 电脑 上 也不配置D型 口。

Yīncǐ, shèbèi chǎngshāng tígōng USB kǒu dēnglù fāngshì, bù xūyào ānzhuāng rènhé qūdòng,
因此, 设备 厂商 提供 USB 口登录方式, 不需要 安装 任何驱动,

gěi wǎngluò gōngchéngshī tiáoshì shèbèi tígōngle hěn dà fāngbiàn.
给 网络 工程师 调试设备提供了很大方便。

Log-in Method through USB Port

The Console port was the 9-pin D-type port on the computer terminal in the past. Now, D-type ports are generally not configured not only on laptops, but also on many desktop computers. Therefore, device manufacturers provide the log-in method through USB port, which does not require the installation of any drivers, providing great convenience for network engineers to debug the device.

补充专业词语 bǔchōng zhuānyè cíyǔ Supplementary Specialized Vocabulary 🎧 02-07

| 1. | 串口线 | chuànkǒuxiàn | phr. | serial line |
| 2. | 标签栏 | biāoqiānlán | phr. | tab bar |

第二部分 Part 2
汉字 Chinese Characters

一、汉字知识 Hànzì zhīshi Knowledge about Chinese Characters

1. 汉字的笔画（2） **Strokes of Chinese characters (2)**

笔画 Strokes	名称 Names	例字 Examples
丶	点 diǎn	六
ㄱ	横折 héngzhé	口、日、五
ㄴ	竖折 shùzhé	山
ㄥ	撇折 piězhé	么

2. 汉字的笔顺（2） **Stroke orders of Chinese characters (2)**

规则 Rules	例字 Examples	笔顺 Stroke orders
先上后下 Upper strokes before lower strokes	三	一 二 三
先左后右 Left-side strokes before right-side strokes	人	丿 人

二、汉字认读与书写 Hànzì rèndú yǔ shūxiě The Recognition and Writing of Chinese Characters

认读下列汉字构成的词语，并试着写汉字。
Read the words composed of the following Chinese characters, and try to write them.

设备管理器   线缆   端口   登录

设		备			管			理	
器		线			缆			端	
口		登			录				

第三部分　Part 3

日常用语 Daily Expressions

① 最近怎么样？ Zuìjìn zěnmeyàng? How are you doing these days?
② 认识您很高兴。 Rènshi nín hěn gāoxìng. Nice to meet you.

第四部分　Part 4

单元实训 Unit Practical Training

dānyuán shíxùn
单元实训
Unit Practical Training

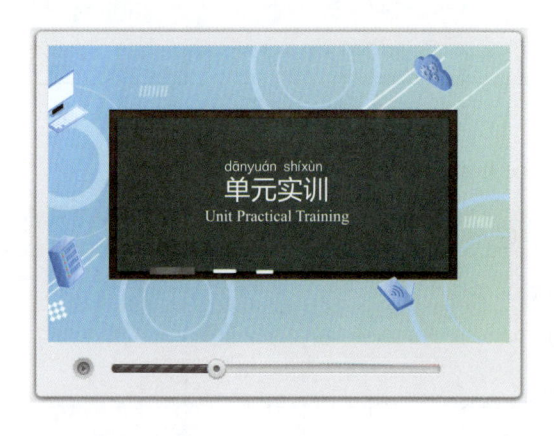

通过 Console 口登录设备 Log in to the Device through the Console Port

实训目的 Training purpose

掌握通过 Console 口登录设备的方法和步骤，培养团队合作精神。

To master the methods and steps of logging in to the device through the Console port, and cultivate the spirit of teamwork.

通过 Console 口登录设备
Log in to the Device through the Console Port

实训组织 Training organization

每组 4 人，选出一个组长。

Students work in groups of 4. Each group chooses a group leader.

实训内容 Training content

通过 Console 口登录设备。

Logging in to the device through the Console port.

实训步骤 Training steps

❶ 将参加人员分成若干小组，每组 4 人。

Divide the students into groups of 4.

❷ 第一个人负责电脑与设备的连接。

The first student is responsible for the connection of the computer and the device.

❸ 第二个人负责配置电脑侧通信软件，实现网络设备与电脑侧通信成功。

The second student is responsible for configuring the communication software on the computer side to realize successful communication between the network device and the computer side.

❹ 实训结束，总结评价。

The teacher makes a summary and an evaluation, and ends the training.

第五部分　Part 5　单元小结 Unit Summary

cíyǔ 词语 Vocabulary

普通词语　General Vocabulary

1.	通过	tōngguò	prep.	through
2.	实现	shíxiàn	v.	realize
3.	与	yǔ	conj.	and
4.	为什么	wèi shénme	phr.	why
5.	这样	zhèyàng	pron.	such
6.	因为	yīnwèi	conj.	because
7.	初始	chūshǐ	n.	inception, initial stage
8.	状态	zhuàngtài	n.	state
9.	下	xià	n.	being in
10.	没有	méiyǒu	v.	not have
11.	只	zhǐ	adv.	only
12.	用	yòng	v.	use
13.	根	gēn	m.	*a measure word for something long and thin*
14.	一端	yì duān	phr.	one end

25

词语 Vocabulary

15.	插	chā	v.	plug
16.	侧	cè	n.	side
17.	上	shang	n.	upside
18.	另	lìng	pron.	other
19.	所有	suǒyǒu	adj.	all
20.	都	dōu	adv.	all, both
21.	必备	bìbèi	v.	be necessary
22.	接口	jiēkǒu	n.	interface

专业词语 Specialized Vocabulary

1.	Console 口	Console kǒu	phr.	Console port
	口	kǒu	n.	port
2.	设备端	shèbèiduān	phr.	on-device, device side
3.	USB 口	USB kǒu	phr.	USB port

补充专业词语 Supplementary Specialized Vocabulary

1.	串口线	chuànkǒuxiàn	phr.	serial line
2.	标签栏	biāoqiānlán	phr.	tab bar

句子 Sentences

1. 通过 Console 口登录设备，就是通过网络设备的 Console 口实现设备与电脑的通信。
2. 连接网络设备与电脑，需要用一根 Console 线缆来连接，一端插在电脑侧的 USB 口上，另一端插在设备的 Console 口上。

3

Shèbèi de jīběn pèizhì
设备的基本配置
Basic Configuration of the Device

---

pèizhì shèbèi jiēkǒu IP dìzhǐ de zhǐlìng
配置 设备 接口 IP 地址 的 指令
Instructions to Configure the Device Interface's IP Address

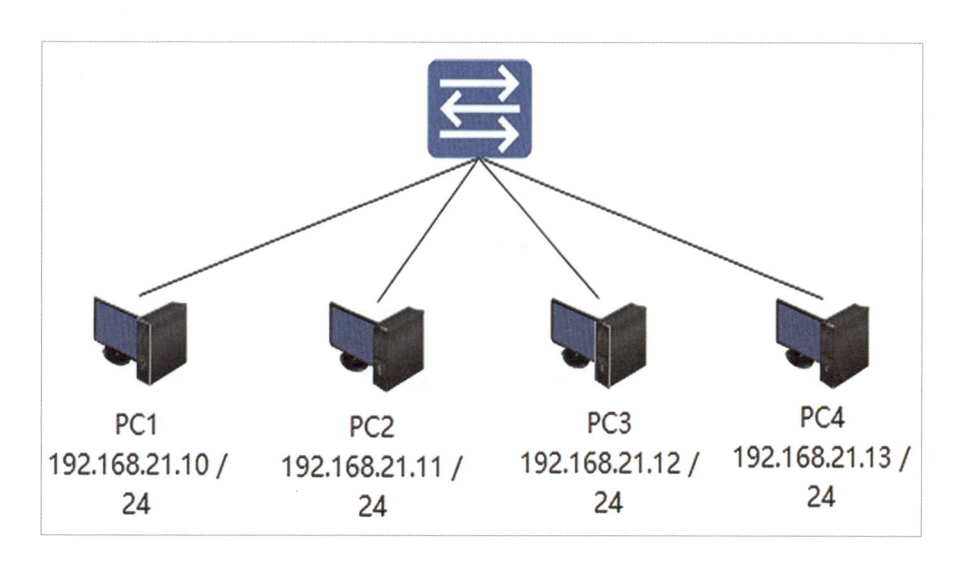

PC1
192.168.21.10 / 24

PC2
192.168.21.11 / 24

PC3
192.168.21.12 / 24

PC4
192.168.21.13 / 24

yí gè shèbèi jiēkǒu pèizhì yí gè IP dìzhǐ
一个 设备 接口 配置 一个 IP 地址
one device interface is configured with one IP address

```
<Huawei>system-view
Enter system view, return user view with Ctrl+Z.
<Huawei> ip address 10.1.1.100 255.255.255.0
```

Shèzhì IP dìzhǐ wéi 10.1.1.100/24 de shèzhì zhǐlìng wéi ip address 10.1.1.100 255.255.255.0.
设置 IP 地址为 10.1.1.100/24 的设置 指令 为 ip address 10.1.1.100 255.255.255.0。
  Qízhōng, IP dìzhǐ wéi 10.1.1.100, zǐwǎng yǎnmǎ wéi 255.255.255.0.
  其中，IP 地址为 10.1.1.100，子网 掩码 为 255.255.255.0。
The setting instruction for setting the IP address 10.1.1.100/24 is 10.1.1.100 255.255.255.0, among which the IP address is 10.1.1.100, and the subnet mask is 255.255.255.0

题解 Introduction

1. 学习内容：设备名称、时区、系统时间和IP地址的配置。
   Learning content: The configuration of the name, time zone, system time and IP address of the device.
2. 知识目标：掌握设备基本配置过程中的核心词汇，学习汉字的笔画"㇆、亅、丿、乚"、笔顺"先中间后两边、先外边后里边"和结构，学写相关汉字。
   Knowledge objectives: To master the core vocabulary used in the basic configuration process of the device, learn the strokes "㇆、亅、丿、乚" and the stroke order "strokes in the middle before those on both sides, outside strokes before inside strokes" and the structures of Chinese characters, and write the related characters.
3. 技能目标：学会配置设备名称、时区、系统时间和IP地址。
   Skill objective: To learn to configure the name, time zone, system time and IP address of the device.

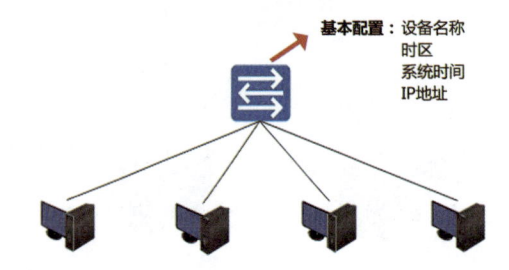

第一部分 Part 1

课文 Texts

一、热身 rèshēn Warm-up

1. 请给词语选择对应的图片。 Choose the corresponding pictures for the words.

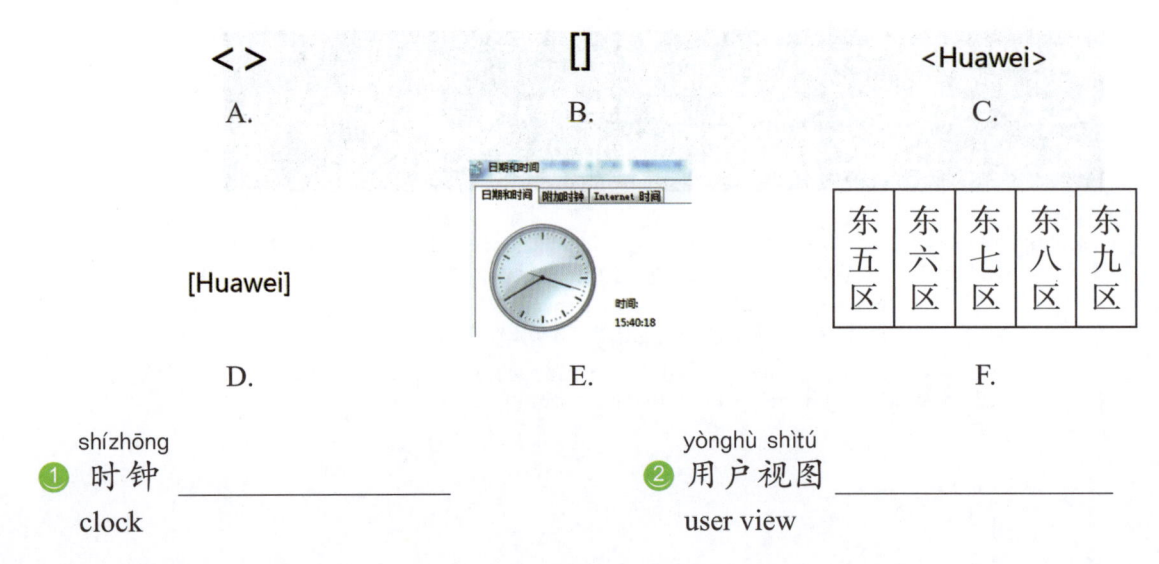

A. < >　　B. [ ]　　C. <Huawei>

D. [Huawei]　　E. (clock image)　　F. 东五区 东六区 东七区 东八区 东九区

① shízhōng 时钟 _____ clock

② yònghù shìtú 用户视图 _____ user view

3 设备的基本配置
Basic Configuration of the Device

③ jiānkuòhào
尖括号_____
angle brackets

④ fāngkuòhào
方括号_____
square brackets

⑤ Zhōngguó shíqū
中国 时区_____
time zone of China

⑥ xìtǒng shìtú
系统视图_____
system view

2. 观看介绍命令行界面中视图的三种分类的视频，并按视频讲解的先后顺序将它们排序。
   Watch the video introducing the three categories of views in the command line interface, and arrange them in order to the video.

minglínghàng jièmiàn zhōng shìtú
命令行界面中视图
de sān zhǒng fēnlèi
的三种分类
Three Categories of Views in the Command Line Interface

A. jiēkǒu shìtú
   接口视图
   interface view

B. yònghù shìtú
   用户视图
   user view

C. xìtǒng shìtú
   系统视图
   system view

① _____   ② _____   ③ _____

二、课文 kèwén Texts

A 🎧 03-01

kèwén A
课文 A
Text A

29

徒弟：师傅，命令行界面中的尖括号"< >"和方括号"[ ]"里面的内容是什么？

师傅：尖括号"< >"或方括号"[ ]"中是设备的名称，也称为"设备主机名"。缺省情况下，设备名称为"Huawei"。

徒弟：它们有什么区别？

师傅：例如 <Huawei> 是用户视图，[Huawei] 是系统视图。

徒弟：那这两种视图如何切换？

师傅：在用户视图下输入"system-view"命令进入系统视图，在系统视图下按"Ctrl+Z"键返回用户视图。

```
<Huawei>system-view
Enter system view, return user view with Ctrl+Z.
[Huawei]
<Huawei>
```

<Huawei> —System-view→ [Huawei]
         ←Ctrl+Z—

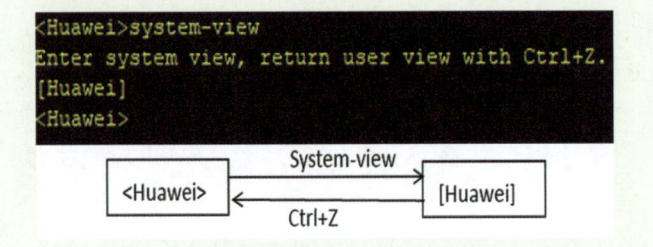

译文 yìwén Text in English

Apprentice: Master, what are the contents in the angle brackets "< >" and square brackets "[]" in the command line interface?

Master: In angle brackets "< >" or square brackets "[]" there is the name of the device, also known as "device host name". By default, the device name is "Huawei".

Apprentice: What are their differences?

Master: For example, < Huawei > is the user view and [Huawei] is the system view.

Apprentice: How to switch between these two views?

Master: Enter the "system-view" command in the user view to enter the system view, and press "Ctrl + Z" keys in the system view to return to the user view.

普通词语 pǔtōng cíyǔ General Vocabulary 🎧 03-02

1.	尖括号	jiānkuòhào	phr.	angle bracket
	括号	kuòhào	n.	bracket
2.	方括号	fāngkuòhào	phr.	square bracket
3.	内容	nèiróng	n.	content
4.	或	huò	conj.	or
5.	名称	míngchēng	n.	name
6.	称为	chēngwéi	phr.	be named
7.	缺省	quēshěng	v.	default
8.	情况	qíngkuàng	n.	situation, condition
9.	它们	tāmen	pron.	they
10.	例如	lìrú	v.	quote an example
11.	切换	qiēhuàn	v.	switch
12.	进入	jìnrù	v.	enter
13.	按	àn	v.	press
14.	键	jiàn	n.	key
15.	返回	fǎnhuí	v.	return

专业词语 zhuānyè cíyǔ Specialized Vocabulary 🎧 03-03

1.	主机名	zhǔjīmíng	phr.	host name
2.	用户视图	yònghù shìtú	phr.	user view

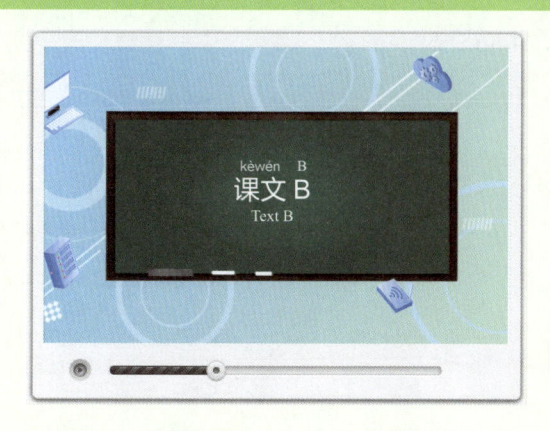

B 🎧 03-04

课文 B
Text B

túdì: Shīfu, qǐngwèn Huáwéi shèbèi chūchǎng shí cǎiyòng shénme shízhōng?
徒弟：师傅，请问 华为设备 出厂 时采用 什么 时钟？

shīfu: Cǎiyòng de shì xiétiáo shìjièshí, yě jiù shì shìjiè tǒngyī shíjiān.
师傅：采用 的是协调世界时，也就是世界统一时间。

túdì 徒弟:	Wǒmen shǐyòng shí, rúhé pèizhì shèbèi xìtǒng shízhōng? 我们使用时,如何配置设备系统时钟?			
shīfu 师傅:	Zài pèizhì shèbèi shízhōng qián, xūyào liǎojiě shèbèi suǒ zài de shíqū bìng jìnxíng pèizhì. 在配置设备时钟前,需要了解设备所在的时区并进行配置。			
	Shèzhì hǎo shíqū hòu, jiù kěyǐ shèzhì shèbèi dāngqián de rìqī hé shíjiān le. 设置好时区后,就可以设置设备当前的日期和时间了。			
túdì 徒弟:	Huáwéi shèbèi zhīchí 12 xiǎoshízhì háishi 24 xiǎoshízhì? 华为设备支持12小时制还是24小时制?			
shīfu 师傅:	Huáwéi shèbèi jǐn zhīchí 24 xiǎoshízhì. 华为设备仅支持24小时制。			

```
<Huawei>clock timezone BJ add 08:00
<Huawei>clock datetime 09:36:00 2021-07-16
<Huawei>display clock
2021-07-16 09:36:06
Friday
Time Zone(BJ) : UTC+08:00
```

译文 yìwén Text in English

Apprentice: Master, what clock does Huawei device adopt when leaving the factory?

Master: It adopts coordinated universal time, i.e. UTC.

Apprentice: How do we configure the device's system clock when we use it?

Master: Before configuring the device clock, you need to know the time zone of the device and configure it. After setting the time zone, you can set the current date and time of the device.

Apprentice: Does Huawei device support 12-hour system or 24-hour system?

Master: Huawei device only supports 24-hour system.

普通词语 pǔtōng cíyǔ General Vocabulary 03-05

1.	出厂	chū//chǎng	v.	(of products) be dispatched from the factory
2.	时	shí	n.	(the duration of) time
3.	采用	cǎiyòng	v.	adopt
4.	时钟	shízhōng	n.	clock
5.	世界	shìjiè	n.	world
6.	统一	tǒngyī	adj.	universal, unified
7.	时间	shíjiān	n.	time
8.	了解	liǎojiě	v.	understand
9.	所	suǒ	part.	used before the verb to indicate the receiver of the action

10.	在	zài	v.	be in/on/at
11.	进行	jìnxíng	v.	proceed
12.	当前	dāngqián	n.	current time, present
13.	日期	rìqī	n.	date
14.	支持	zhīchí	v.	support
15.	小时制	xiǎoshízhì	phr.	hour system
16.	仅	jǐn	adv.	only

专业词语 zhuānyè cíyǔ Specialized Vocabulary 🎧 03-06

1.	协调世界时	xiétiáo shìjièshí	phr.	coordinated universal time
	协调	xiétiáo	v./adj.	coordinate; coordinated
	世界时	shìjièshí	n.	universal time
2.	系统时钟	xìtǒng shízhōng	phr.	system clock
3.	时区	shíqū	n.	time zone

三、视听说 shì-tīng-shuō Viewing, Listening and Speaking

1. 观看介绍配置设备的时区和时间的方法的视频，将正确的配置指令填在横线上。
Watch the video introducing the methods of configuring the time zone and time of the device, and fill in the blanks with correct configuration instructions.

配置设备的时区和时间的方法
pèizhì shèbèi de shíqū hé shíjiān de fāngfǎ
Methods of Configuring the Time Zone and Time of the Device

A. <Huawei>system-view
B. <NIIT_R1>clock timezone BJ add 08:00
C. [Huawei]sysname NIIT_R1 [NIIT_R1]
D. <NIIT_R1>clock datetime 01:04:00 2021-6-10

❶ Jiǎshè shèbèi wèiyú Běijīng, zé xiāngyìng de pèizhì zhǐlìng yīnggāi shì:
假设设备位于北京，则相应的配置指令应该是：＿＿＿＿＿＿＿＿
Assuming that the device is located in Beijing, the corresponding configuration instructions should be

❷ 假设当前的日期为2021年6月10日，时间是凌晨01:04:00，则相应的配置指令应该是：_____

Assuming that the current date is June 10, 2021 and the time is 01:04:00 a.m., then the corresponding configuration instructions should be

2. 说一说 Let's talk.

说一说如何配置设备的时区和时间。 Talk about how to configure the time zone and time of the device.

四、学以致用 xuéyǐzhìyòng Practicing What You Have Learnt

观看介绍为设备接口配置 IP 地址的视频，并根据视频操作，为下面的问题选择正确的答案。
Watch the video about configuring the IP address for the device interface, and choose the correct answers for the following questions based on the operations in the video.

A. 255.255.255.0
B. 255.0.0.0
C. ip address 10.1.1.100 255.255.255.0
D. 10.1.1.100
E. 10.1.1.0

IP 地址为 10.1.1.100/24 的设置指令为 ❶_____，其中 IP 地址为 ❷_____，
The setting instructions for IP address 10.1.1.100/24 is   among which the IP address is

子网掩码为 ❸_____。
and the subnet mask is

五、小知识 xiǎo zhīshi Tips

如何登录到设备命令行界面
Rúhé dēnglù dào shèbèi mìnglìngháng jièmiàn

用户可以通过不同的方式登录到设备命令行界面，包括 Console 口登录、MiniUSB 口登录以及 Telnet 登录。首次登录新设备时，由于新设备为空配置设备，所以只能通过 Console 口或 MiniUSB 口登录。首次登录到新设备后，便可以给设备配置一个 IP 地址，然后开启 Telnet 功能。

How to Log in to the Device Command Line Interface

Users can log in to the device command line interface in different ways, including Console port login, MiniUSB port login and Telnet login. When logging in to a new device for the first time, because the device is an unconfigured one, it can only be logged in through the Console port or MiniUSB port. After logging in to the new device for the first time, you can configure an IP address for the device, and then turn on the Telnet function.

补充专业词语 bǔchōng zhuānyè cíyǔ Supplementary Specialized Vocabulary 🎧 03-07

#	词语	拼音	词性	英文
1.	配置指令	pèizhì zhǐlìng	phr.	configuration instruction
2.	中国时区	Zhōngguó shíqū	phr.	time zone of China

第二部分 Part 2
汉字 Chinese Characters

一、汉字知识 Hànzì zhīshi Knowledge about Chinese Characters

1. 汉字的笔画（3） Strokes of Chinese characters (3)

笔画 Strokes	名称 Names	例字 Examples
㇇	横钩 hénggōu	买
亅	竖钩 shùgōu	小
㇉	弯钩 wāngōu	子
㇄	竖弯钩 shùwāngōu	七

2. 汉字的笔顺（3） Stroke orders of Chinese characters (3)

规则 Rules	例字 Examples	笔顺 Stroke orders
先中间后两边 Strokes in the middle before those on both sides	小	亅 小 小
先外边后里边 Outside strokes before inside strokes	月、问	丿 冂 月 月 丶 冂 冂 问 问

二、汉字认读与书写　Hànzì rèndú yǔ shūxiě　The Recognition and Writing of Chinese Characters

认读下列汉字构成的词语，并试着写汉字。
Read the words composed of the following Chinese characters, and try to write them.

用户视图　配置指令　尖括号　主机名

用				户				视				图			
配				置				指				令			
尖				括				号				主			
机				名											

第三部分　Part 3

日常用语　Daily Expressions

❶ 我来介绍一下，这位是李伟先生。Wǒ lái jièshào yíxià, zhè wèi shì Lǐ Wěi xiānsheng. Let me make an introduction. This is Mr. Li Wei.

❷ 请问，南京饭店在哪儿？Qǐngwèn, Nánjīng Fàndiàn zài nǎr? Excuse me, where's Nanjing Hotel?

第四部分 Part 4　单元实训 Unit Practical Training

设备的基本配置 Basic Configuration of the Device

实训目的 Training purpose
掌握设备的基本配置方法。

To master the basic configuration method of the device.

实训组织 Training organization
每组 3～5 人，选出一个组长。

Students work in groups of 3-5. Each group chooses a group leader.

实训内容 Training content
配置设备名称、时区、系统时间、设备的 IP 地址。

Configure the name, time zone, system time and IP address of the device.

实训步骤 Training steps
❶ 配置设备名称为 Niit。

　Configure the device name as Niit.

❷ 设置设备的时区为北京时区。

　Set the time zone of the device to Beijing time zone.

❸ 设置设备的系统时间为当前的时间。

　Set the system time of the device to the current time.

❹ 显示设备时间，验证步骤 2～3 是否设置正确。

　Display the device time to verify whether steps 2-3 are set correctly.

❺ 配置设备的 IP 地址：假设设备 Niit 的管理接口为 GigabitEthernet 0/0/0，分配的 IP 地址为 10.1.1.60，子网掩码为 255.255.255.0。

　Configure the IP address of the device: Assuming that the management interface of the device Niit is GigabitEthernet 0/0/0, the assigned IP address is 10.1.1.60, and the subnet mask is 255.255.255.0.

❻ 实训结束，总结评价。

　The teacher makes a summary and an evaluation, and ends the training.

第五部分 Part 5　单元小结 Unit Summary

词语 Vocabulary

普通词语　General Vocabulary

1.	尖括号	jiānkuòhào	phr.	angle bracket
	括号	kuòhào	n.	bracket
2.	方括号	fāngkuòhào	phr.	square bracket
3.	内容	nèiróng	n.	content
4.	或	huò	conj.	or
5.	名称	míngchēng	n.	name
6.	称为	chēngwéi	phr.	be named
7.	缺省	quēshěng	v.	default
8.	情况	qíngkuàng	n.	situation, condition
9.	它们	tāmen	pron.	they
10.	例如	lìrú	v.	quote an example
11.	切换	qiēhuàn	v.	switch
12.	进入	jìnrù	v.	enter
13.	按	àn	v.	press
14.	键	jiàn	n.	key
15.	返回	fǎnhuí	v.	return
16.	出厂	chū//chǎng	v.	(of products) be dispatched from the factory
17.	时	shí	n.	(the duration of) time
18.	采用	cǎiyòng	v.	adopt
19.	时钟	shízhōng	n.	clock
20.	世界	shìjiè	n.	world
21.	统一	tǒngyī	adj.	universal, unified
22.	时间	shíjiān	n.	time
23.	了解	liǎojiě	v.	understand
24.	所	suǒ	part.	used before the verb to indicate the receiver of the action
25.	在	zài	v.	be in/on/at
26.	进行	jìnxíng	v.	proceed
27.	当前	dāngqián	n.	current time, present
28.	日期	rìqī	n.	date

词语 Vocabulary

29.	支持	zhīchí	v.	support
30.	小时制	xiǎoshízhì	phr.	hour system
31.	仅	jǐn	adv.	only

专业词语　Specialized Vocabulary

1.	主机名	zhǔjīmíng	phr.	host name
2.	用户视图	yònghù shìtú	phr.	user view
3.	协调世界时	xiétiáo shìjièshí	phr.	coordinated universal time
	协调	xiétiáo	v./adj.	coordinate; coordinated
	世界时	shìjièshí	n.	universal time
4.	系统时钟	xìtǒng shízhōng	phr.	system clock
5.	时区	shíqū	n.	time zone

补充专业词语　Supplementary Specialized Vocabulary

1.	配置指令	pèizhì zhǐlìng	phr.	configuration instruction
2.	中国时区	Zhōngguó shíqū	phr.	time zone of China

句子 Sentences

1. 尖括号"< >"或方括号"[ ]"中是设备的名称，也称为"设备主机名"。缺省情况下，设备名称为"Huawei"。
2. 例如 <Huawei> 是用户视图，[Huawei] 是系统视图。
3. 在用户视图下输入"system-view"命令进入系统视图，在系统视图下按"Ctrl＋Z"键返回用户视图。
4. 在配置设备时钟前，需要了解设备所在的时区并进行配置。设置好时区后，就可以设置设备当前的日期和时间了。
5. 华为设备仅支持 24 小时制。

4

Yònghù jièmiàn pèizhì
用户界面配置
Configuration of User Interface

VTY yònghù jièmiàn pèizhì de bùzhòu
VTY 用户 界面 配置 的步骤
Steps of Configuring VTY User Interface

```
[Huawei]user-interface maximum-vty 15
```

pèizhì zuì dà VTY yònghù jièmiàn shù wéi 15
1. 配置 最大 VTY 用户 界面 数 为 15
Configure the maximun number of VTY user interfaces as 15.

```
[Huawei]user-interface vty 0 14
```

jìnrù VTY yònghù jièmiàn shìtú
2. 进入 VTY 用户 界面 视图
Enter the VTY user interface view.

```
[Huawei-ui-vty 0-14]authentication-mode aaa
```

pèizhì rènzhèng fāngshì wéi AAA
3. 配置 认证 方式 为 AAA
Configure the authentication method as AAA.

```
[Huawei-aaa]local-user ORK password cipher waaaagh
```

pèizhì AAA yònghùmíng hé mìmǎ
4. 配置 AAA 用户名 和 密码
Configure the AAA user name and password.

```
[Huawei-aaa]local-user ORK service-type telnet
```

pèizhì yònghù kě fǎngwèn de yèwù lèixíng
5. 配置 用户 可 访问 的 业务 类型
Configure the service types accessible to the user.

41

题解　Introduction

1. 学习内容：用户界面的含义及用户界面配置的步骤。
   Learning content: The meaning of the user interface and the steps of configuring the user interface.
2. 知识目标：掌握用户界面配置中关键步骤的核心词语，学习汉字的笔画"㇏、丨、乛、乚"、笔顺"先里头，后封口"和结构，学写相关汉字。
   Knowledge objectives: To master the core vocabulary used in the key steps of configuring the user interface, learn the strokes "㇏, 丨, 乛, 乚" and the stroke order "outside strokes before inside strokes, and then sealing strokes" and the structures of Chinese characters, and write the related characters.
3. 技能目标：学习并掌握用户界面配置的方法及步骤。
   Skill objective: To learn and master the methods and steps of configuring the user interface.

第一部分　Part 1

课文　Texts

一、热身　rèshēn　Warm-up

1. 下面是 Console 用户界面和 VTY 用户界面图示，请给词语选择对应的图示。
The following are the illustrations of Console and VTY user interfaces. Please choose the corresponding illustrations for the words.

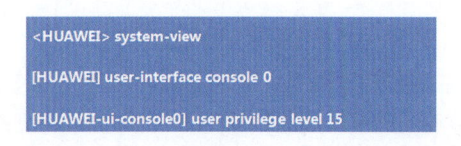

A.　　　　　　　　　　　　　　B.

❶ VTY 用户界面＿＿＿＿＿＿　　❷ Console 用户界面＿＿＿＿＿＿
　VTY yònghù jièmiàn　　　　　　　Console yònghù jièmiàn
　VTY user interface　　　　　　　Console user interface

用户界面配置
Configuration of User Interface 4

2. 观看介绍用户界面信息的视频，将词语填入相应位置。
Watch the video introducing the user interface information, and fill in the corresponding positions with the words.

A. xiāngduì biānhào
相对 编号
relative number

B. juéduì biānhào
绝对 编号
absolute number

C. rènzhèng fāngshì
认证 方式
authentication method

D. yònghù jíbié
用户 级别
user level

```
<Huawei>display user-interface
    Idx  Type  Tx/Rx  Modem Privi ActualPrivi Auth Int
+   0    CON 0  9600    -     15      15       P    -
    129  VTY 0          -     0       -        N    -
    130  VTY 1          -     0       -        N    -
    131  VTY 2          -     0       -        N    -
    132  VTY 3          -     0       -        N    -
    133  VTY 4          -     0       -        N    -
    145  VTY 16         -     0       -        N    -
    146  VTY 17         -     0       -        N    -
    147  VTY 18         -     0       -        N    -
    148  VTY 19         -     0       -        N    -
    149  VTY 20         -     0       -        N    -
```

二、课文 kèwén Texts

A 04-01

课文 A
kèwén A
Text A

túdì: Shīfu, shénme shì yònghù jièmiàn?
徒弟：师傅，什么是用户界面？

43

shīfu: Yònghù zài yǔ shèbèi jìnxíng tōngxìn de guòchéng zhōng, bù tóng de yònghù yōngyǒu shǔyú zìjǐ de jièmiàn.
师傅：用户在与设备进行通信的过程中，不同的用户拥有属于自己的界面。

túdì: Yònghù jièmiàn yǒu shénme zuòyòng ne?
徒弟：用户界面有什么作用呢？

shīfu: Měi gè yònghù jièmiàn dōu yǒu yí xìliè shǔxìng, tōngguò shèzhì yònghù jièmiàn shǔxìng kěyǐ kòngzhì yònghù de xíngwéi, bǐrú rènzhèng fāngshì、yònghù jíbié děng.
师傅：每个用户界面都有一系列属性，通过设置用户界面属性可以控制用户的行为，比如认证方式、用户级别等。

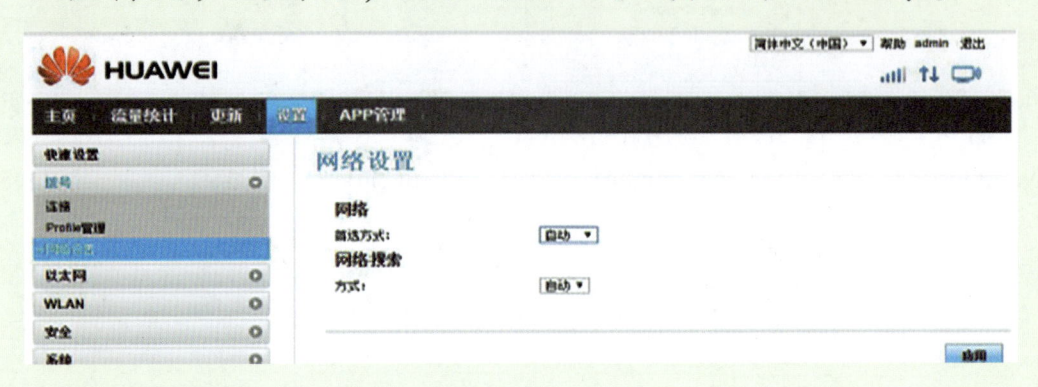

译文 yìwén Text in English

Apprentice: Master, what is a user interface?

Master: Different users have their own interfaces during the process of communicating with devices.

Apprentice: What is the user interface used for?

Master: Each user interface has a series of attributes. The user interface attributes can be set to control the user's behavior, such as authentication mode and user level, etc.

普通词语 pǔtōng cíyǔ General Vocabulary 04-02

1.	过程	guòchéng	n.	process
2.	不同	bù tóng	phr.	different
3.	拥有	yōngyǒu	v.	own
4.	属于	shǔyú	v.	belong to
5.	自己	zìjǐ	pron.	oneself
6.	每个	měi gè	phr.	every
	每	měi	pron.	each
7.	系列	xìliè	n.	series
8.	控制	kòngzhì	v.	control

44

| 9. | 行为 | xíngwéi | n. | behavior |
| 10. | 比如 | bǐrú | v. | take sth. for example |

专业词语 zhuānyè cíyǔ Specialized Vocabulary 🎧 04-03

1.	用户界面	yònghù jièmiàn	phr.	user interface
2.	认证方式	rènzhèng fāngshì	phr.	authentication mode
	认证	rènzhèng	v.	authenticate, certify
	方式	fāngshì	n.	mode

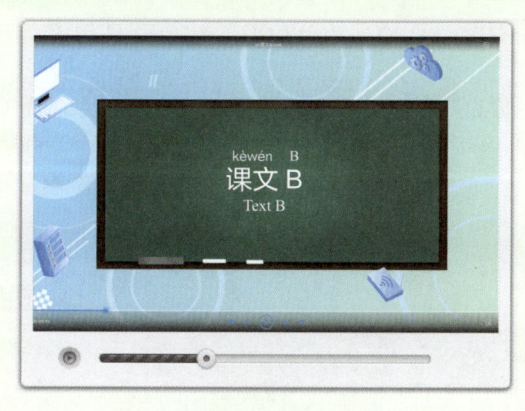

B 🎧 04-04

课文 B
Text B

túdì: Shīfu, shénme shì VTY yònghù jièmiàn?
徒弟：师傅，什么是 VTY 用户界面？

shīfu: Shì shǐyòng Telnet fāngshì dēnglù de yònghù jièmiàn.
师傅：是使用 Telnet 方式登录的用户界面。

túdì: VTY yònghù jièmiàn rúhé pèizhì?
徒弟：VTY 用户界面如何配置？

shīfu: Shǒuxiān, jìnrù VTY yònghù jièmiàn shìtú; ránhòu, pèizhì rènzhèng fāngshì wéi password; zuìhòu, pèizhì yònghù dēnglù mìmǎ.
师傅：首先，进入 VTY 用户界面视图；然后，配置认证方式为 password；最后，配置用户登录密码。

```
[Huawei]user-interface vty ?
  INTEGER<0-4>  The first user terminal interface to be configured

[Huawei]user-interface vty 0 4
[Huawei-ui-vty0-4]
```

译文 yìwén Text in English

Apprentice: Master, what is a VTY user interface?

Master: It is the user interface that uses Telnet to login.

Apprentice: How to configure the VTY user interface?

Master: First, enter the VTY user interface view, then configure the authentication mode as password, and finally configure the user login password.

专业词语 zhuānyè cíyǔ Specialized Vocabulary 🎧 04-05

| VTY 用户界面 | VTY yònghù jièmiàn | phr. | VTY user interface |

三、视听说 shì-tīng-shuō Viewing, Listening and Speaking

1. 观看介绍 VTY 用户界面配置的视频，将每个配置步骤与其对应的含义连线。

Watch the video about configuring VTY user interface, and connect each configuration step to its corresponding meaning.

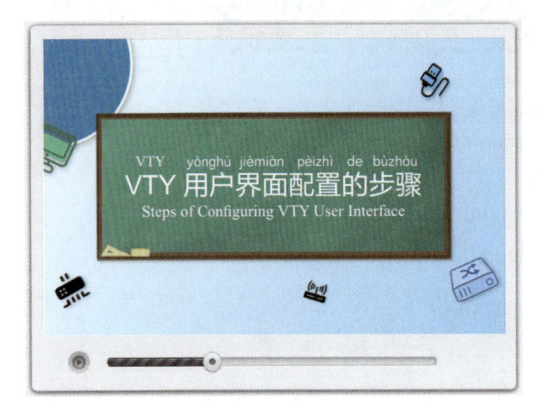

46

用户界面配置
Configuration of User Interface 4

❶ <Huawei> system-view [Huawei] user-interface maximum-vty 15

❷ [Huawei] user-interface vty 0 14

❸ [Huawei-ui-vty0-14] authentication-mode aaa

❹ [Huawei-ui-vty0-14] quit[Huawei] aaa[Huawei-aaa] local-user admin password cipher admin@123

❺ [Huawei-aaa] local-user admin service-type telnet[Huawei-aaa] quit

A. 进入 VTY 用户界面视图
enter the VTY user interface view

B. 配置最大 VTY 用户界面数为 15
configure the maximum number of VTY user interfaces as 15

C. 配置 AAA 用户名和密码
configure the AAA user name and password

D. 配置用户可访问的业务类型
configure the service types accessible to the user

E. 配置认证方式为 AAA
configure the authentication mode as AAA

2. 说一说 Let's talk.

说一说 VTY 用户界面配置步骤的含义。
Talk about the meanings of the steps to configure VTY user interface.

四、学以致用 xuéyǐzhìyòng Practicing What You Have Learnt

观看介绍 VTY 用户界面配置的视频，请在每个操作下面填入对应的汉语。
Watch the video about configuring VTY user interface, and fill in the corresponding Chinese under each operation.

VTY 用户界面配置
操作的含义
Meanings of the Operations to Configure VTY User Interface

[Huawei-ui-vty0-14]idle-timeout
❶ _____

[Huawei]user-interface maximum-vty
❷ _____

47

```
[Huawei]user-interface vty 0 14
          ③ _____
[Huawei-ui-vty16-20]user privilege level ?
  INTEGER<0-15>   Set a priority
          ④ _____
[Huawei-ui-vty16-20]authentication-mode
          ⑤ _____
[Huawei-ui-vty16-20]set authentication password
          ⑥ _____
```

A. shèzhì rènzhèng fāngshì
设置 认证 方式
set the authentication mode

B. shèzhì rènzhèng mìmǎ
设置 认证 密码
set the authentication password

C. jìnrù yònghù jièmiàn shìtú
进入用户界面视图
enter the user interface view

D. shèzhì yònghù jíbié
设置用户级别
set the user level

E. shèzhì zuì dà VTY shùmù
设置最大 VTY 数目
set the maximum VTY number

F. shèzhì yònghù jièmiàn chāoshí shícháng
设置用户界面超时 时长
set the user interface timeout value

五、小知识   xiǎo zhīshi   Tips

VTY yònghù jièmiàn yǔ Console yònghù jièmiàn
VTY 用户界面与 Console 用户界面

VTY yònghù jièmiàn duìyìng yú shǐyòng Telnet fāngshì dēnglù de yònghù。 Console yònghù
VTY 用户界面对应于使用 Telnet 方式登录的用户。Console 用户

jièmiàn duìyìng yú cóng Console kǒu dēnglù de yònghù。 Měi gè yònghù dēnglù shèbèi hòu, duìyìng
界面对应于从 Console 口登录的用户。每个用户登录设备后，对应

yí gè yònghù jièmiàn, tōngguò juéduì biānhào lái jìnxíng wéiyī biāoshí。 Měi gè yònghù jièmiàn duìyìng
一个用户界面，通过绝对 编号来进行唯一标识。每个用户界面对应

yí xìliè de shǔxìng lái kòngzhì gāi yònghù de quánxiàn。
一系列的属性来控制 该 用户的权限。

VTY User Interface and Console User Interface

The VTY user interface corresponds to the user logging in to the device using Telnet. The Console user interface corresponds to the user logging in to the device through the Console port. When each user logs in to the device, he/she has a unique user interface and is uniquely identified with an absolute number. Each user interface corresponds to a series of attributes to control the user's permissions.

4 用户界面配置
Configuration of User Interface

补充专业词语 bǔchōng zhuānyè cíyǔ Supplementary Specialized Vocabulary 🎧 04-06

1.	相对编号	xiāngduì biānhào	phr.	relative number
	编号	biānhào	n.	number
2.	绝对编号	juéduì biānhào	phr.	absolute number
3.	权限	quánxiàn	n.	permission

第二部分 Part 2
汉字 Chinese Characters

一、汉字知识 Hànzì zhīshi Knowledge about Chinese Characters

1. 汉字的笔画（4） Strokes of Chinese characters (4)

笔画 Strokes	名称 Names	例字 Examples
✓	提 tí	习
↳	竖提 shùtí	衣
㇋	横折提 héngzhétí	语
㇏	撇点 piědiǎn	女

2. 汉字的笔顺（4） Stroke orders of Chinese characters (4)

规则 Rule	例字 Examples	笔顺 Stroke orders
先外后里再封口 Outside strokes before inside strokes, and then sealing strokes	国 日	丨 冂 冂 冋 囝 国 国 国 丨 冂 月 日

二、汉字认读与书写 Hànzì rèndú yǔ shūxiě The Recognition and Writing of Chinese Characters

认读下列汉字构成的词语，并试着写汉字。

Read the words composed of the following Chinese characters, and try to write them.

用户级别　　视图

用			户			级			别		
视			图								

49

第三部分　Part 3　日常用语 Daily Expressions

❶ 我们机场见。Wǒmen jīchǎng jiàn. See you at the airport.

❷ 我们电话（邮件）联系。Wǒmen diànhuà (yóujiàn) liánxì. Keep in touch by phone (e-mail).

❸ 下星期一到北京的航班还有票吗？ Xià xīngqīyī dào Běijīng de hángbān hái yǒu piào ma?
Are there any tickets available for next Monday's flight to Beijing?

第四部分　Part 4　单元实训 Unit Practical Training

配置用户界面 Configuring User Interface

实训目的 Training purpose

了解 VTY 用户界面和 Console 用户界面的配置方法和步骤，培养团队合作精神。

To learn the methods and steps of configuring the VTY and Console user interfaces, and cultivate the spirit of teamwork.

实训组织 Training organization

每组 3 人，选出一个组长。

Students work in groups of 3. Each group chooses a group leader.

实训内容 Training content

使用网络模拟器配置 VTY 用户界面和 Console 用户界面。

Using the network simulator to configure the VTY and the Console user interfaces.

实训步骤 Training steps

❶ 将参加人员分成若干组，每组 3 人。

　　Divide the students into groups of 3.

❷ 第一个人负责配置 VTY 用户界面。

　　The first student is responsible for configuring the VTY user interface.

❸ 第二个人负责配置 Console 用户界面。

The second student is responsible for configuring the Console user interface.

❹ 第三个人负责检查第一个人和第二个人的配置是否正确，保存拓扑及配置，将拓扑文件交组长检查。

The third student is responsible for checking whether the configurations made by the first two students are correct. Save the topology and configuration, and submit the topology file to the group leader for inspection.

④ 实训结束，总结评价。

The teacher makes a summary and an evaluation, and ends the training.

第五部分　Part 5　单元小结　Unit Summary

cíyǔ 词语 Vocabulary

普通词语　General Vocabulary

1.	过程	guòchéng	n.	process
2.	不同	bù tóng	phr.	different
3.	拥有	yōngyǒu	v.	own
4.	属于	shǔyú	v.	belong to
5.	自己	zìjǐ	pron.	oneself
6.	每个	měi gè	phr.	every
	每	měi	pron.	each
7.	系列	xìliè	n.	series
8.	控制	kòngzhì	v.	control
9.	行为	xíngwéi	n.	behavior
10.	比如	bǐrú	v.	take sth. for example

专业词语　Specialized Vocabulary

1.	用户界面	yònghù jièmiàn	phr.	user interface
2.	认证方式	rènzhèng fāngshì	phr.	authentication mode
	认证	rènzhèng	v.	authenticate, certify
	方式	fāngshì	n.	mode
3.	VTY 用户界面	VTY yònghù jièmiàn	phr.	VTY user interface

cíyǔ 词语 Vocabulary

补充专业词语　Supplementary Specialized Vocabulary

1.	相对编号	xiāngduì biānhào	phr.	relative number
	编号	biānhào	n.	number
2.	绝对编号	juéduì biānhào	phr.	absolute number
3.	权限	quánxiàn	n.	permission

jùzi 句子 Sentences

1. 用户界面是指用户在与设备进行通信的过程中，不同的用户拥有属于自己的界面。
2. 每个用户界面都有一系列属性，通过设置用户界面属性可以控制用户的行为，比如认证方式、用户级别等。
3. VTY 用户界面是使用 Telnet 方式登录的用户界面。
4. 配置 VTY 用户界面的步骤是：首先，进入 VTY 用户界面视图；然后，配置认证方式为 password；最后，配置用户登录密码。

5

Wénjiàn xìtǒng guǎnlǐ
文件系统管理
File System Management

zài lùyóuqì zhōng duì wénjiàn hé mùlù jìnxíng cāozuò
在路由器 中 对 文件和目录进行 操作
Operation on Files and Directories in the Router

yùnxíng eNSP, qǐdòng lùyóuqì
运行 eNSP，启动 路由器
Run eNSP to start the router.

yòng mkdir mìnglìng chuàngjiàn yí gè mùlù, mùlùmíng jiàozuò
用 mkdir 命令 创建 一个目录，目录名 叫作
"mydir"
<Huawei> mkdir mydir.
Create a directory named "mydir" with the mkdir command.

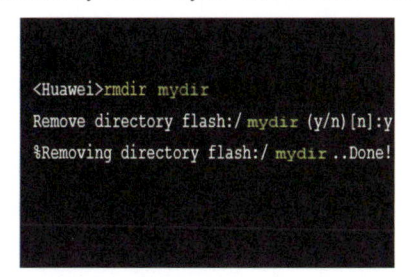

yòng rmdir mìnglìng shānchú mùlù, rú shānchú mydir mùlù
用 rmdir 命令 删除 目录，如 删除 mydir 目录
<Huawei>cd..<Huawei>rmdir mydir
Delete the directory with the rmdir command, for example, deleting the mydir directory: <Huawei>cd..<Huawei> rmdir mydir.

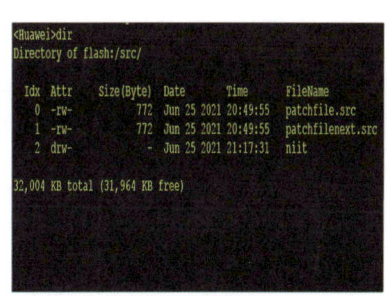

yòng dir mìnglìng, chákàn dāngqián mùlù xià de xìnxī
用 dir 命令，查看 当前 目录下的 信息
Check the information in the current directory with the dir command.

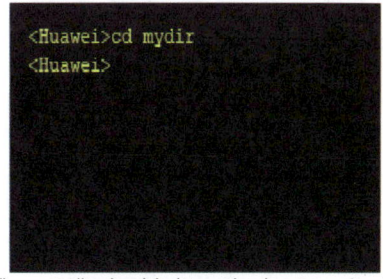

yòng cd mìnglìng xiūgǎi yònghù dāngqián de gōngzuò mùlù wéi mydir
用 cd 命令 修改 用户 当前 的 工作 目录为 mydir
<Huawei>cd mydir
jìnrù mydir mùlù hòu, rúguǒ bù xiǎng yào mydir mùlù le,
（进入 mydir 目录后，如果不 想 要 mydir 目录了，
kěyǐ shānchú.
可以 删除 。）
Change the user's current working directory into mydir: <Huawei>cd mydir.(After entering the mydir directory, if you don't want the mydir directory anymore, you can delete it.)

53

题解　Introduction

1. 学习内容：VRP 文件系统的主要用途及文件系统管理方法。
   Learning content: The main use of the VRP file system and the management method of file systems.

2. 知识目标：掌握文件系统管理中的核心动词，学习汉字的笔画"㇏、㇀、㇁、乚"和独体结构，学写相关汉字。
   Knowledge objectives: To master the core verbs used in the file system management, learn the strokes "㇏、㇀、㇁、乚" and the independent structure of Chinese characters, and write the related characters.

3. 技能目标：会使用目录命令和文件命令对文件进行操作，包括创建目录、显示当前路径、进入指定目录等，以及对文件进行复制、重命名、删除等操作。
   Skill objective: To be able to operate on the files with directory and file commands, including creating directory, displaying the current path, entering a specified directory, and copying, renaming and deleting files, etc.

第一部分　Part 1

课文　Texts

一、热身　rèshēn　Warm-up

1. 下面所给的图示是文件系统管理的标识，请给词语选择对应的图示。
   The following illustrations are the icons of the file system management. Please choose the words for the corresponding illustrations.

   A. 　　　　　　　　　B. 　　　　　　　　　C.

54

文件系统管理 5
File System Management

D. 　　　　　　　　　　　E. 　　　　　　　　　　　F.

   wénjiàn
❶ 文件_____
   file

   mùlù
❷ 目录_____
   directory

   chuàngjiàn
❸ 创建_____
   create

   yídòng
❹ 移动_____
   move

   fùzhì
❺ 复制_____
   copy

   shānchú
❻ 删除_____
   delete

2. 观看介绍 VRP 文件系统主要功能的视频，并把相关内容与其相应的选项匹配。
   Watch the video introducing the main functions of VRP file system, and match the related contents with the corresponding options.

   wénjiàn
❶ 文件
   files

   wàibù cúnchǔqì
A. 外部存储器
   external memory

   Huáwéi lùyóuqì
❷ 华为路由器
   Huawei router

   Flash kǎ
B. Flash 卡
   Flash card

55

中文＋计算机网络技术（中级）

③ jiāohuànjī
交换机
switch

④ mùlù
目录
directory

C. SD kǎ
SD 卡
SD card

D. CF kǎ
CF 卡
CF card

二、课文　kèwén　Texts

A 05-01

课文 A
Text A

túdì:　Mùlù mìnglìng yǒu nǎxiē?
徒弟：目录 命令 有 哪些？

shīfu:　Zhǔyào yǒu xiǎnshì mùlù、chuàngjiàn mùlù、shānchú mùlù、xiǎnshì dāngqián lùjìng、
师傅：主要 有 显示 目录、创建 目录、删除 目录、显示 当前 路径、

　　　jìnrù zhǐdìng mùlù děng mìnglìng.
　　　进入 指定 目录 等 命令。

túdì:　Wénjiàn mìnglìng yǒu nǎxiē?
徒弟：文件 命令 有 哪些？

shīfu:　Zhǔyào yǒu fùzhì wénjiàn、chóng mìngmíng wénjiàn、yídòng wénjiàn、shānchú wénjiàn děng
师傅：主要 有 复制 文件、重 命名 文件、移动 文件、删除 文件 等

　　　mìnglìng.
　　　命令。

56

文件系统管理　5
File System Management

创建
create

删除
delete

译文 yìwén Text in English

Apprentice: What are the directory commands?
Master: They mainly include displaying directory, creating directory, deleting directory, displaying current path and entering specified directory.
Apprentice: What are the file commands?
Master: They mainly include copying, renaming, moving and deleting files.

普通词语 pǔtōng cíyǔ General Vocabulary 🎧 05-02

| 1. | 主要 | zhǔyào | adj. | main |
| 2. | 指定 | zhǐdìng | v. | specify |

专业词语 zhuānyè cíyǔ Specialized Vocabulary 🎧 05-03

1.	目录	mùlù	n.	directory
2.	显示	xiǎnshì	v.	display
3.	删除	shānchú	v.	delete
4.	文件	wénjiàn	n.	file
5.	复制	fùzhì	v.	copy
6.	重命名	chóng mìng//míng	phr.	rename
	重	chóng	adv.	again
	命名	mìng//míng	v.	name
7.	移动	yídòng	v.	move

57

课文 B / Text B

徒弟：师傅，用目录命令可以做什么呢？

师傅：可以显示文件和目录信息，还可以创建和删除目录。

徒弟：还能做其他的吗？

师傅：还可以显示当前路径，或进入一个目录。

徒弟：怎样才能用命令进行操作呢？

师傅：以华为交换机为例，要知道如何启动交换机，并要记住所要使用的命令。比如，进入 src 目录，用 cd src。

华为交换机
Huawei switch

文件系统管理 5
File System Management

译文 yìwén Text in English

Apprentice: Master, what can I do with the directory commands?
Master: You can display file and directory information, and create and delete directories.
Apprentice: Can I do anything else?
Master: You can also display the current path or enter a directory.
Apprentice: How can I operate with the commands?
Master: Taking Huawei switch as an example, you should know how to start the switch, and remember the commands to be used. For example, use cd src to enter the src directory: <Huawei>cd src.

普通词语 pǔtōng cíyǔ General Vocabulary 🎧 05-05

1.	其他	qítā	pron.	other
2.	才	cái	adv.	used to indicate that sth. happens only on certain conditions
3.	以	yǐ	prep.	by, with
4.	例	lì	n.	example
5.	记住	jìzhù	phr.	remember

专业词语 zhuānyè cíyǔ Specialized Vocabulary 🎧 05-06

1.	启动	qǐdòng	v.	start
2.	交换机	jiāohuànjī	n.	switch

三、视听说 shì-tīng-shuō Viewing, Listening and Speaking

1. 观看介绍文件操作的视频，把文件操作命令与对应的中文连线。
Watch the video introducing the operation on the file and connect the file operation commands to the corresponding Chinese.

文件操作及相关的命令
wénjiàn cāozuò jí xiāngguān de mìnglìng
File Operation and Related Commands

59

① fùzhì wénjiàn
复制 文件
copy file

A. <Huawei>move dest.src sub

② chóng mìngmíng wénjiàn
重 命名 文件
rename file

B. <Huawei>rename test.src dest.src

③ yídòng wénjiàn
移动 文件
move file

C. <Huawei>delete dest.src

④ shānchú wénjiàn
删除 文件
delete file

D. <Huawei>copy patchfile.src test.src

2. 说一说 Let's talk.

说一说文件操作命令有哪些。   Talk about the file operation commands.

四、学以致用 xuéyǐzhìyòng Practicing What You Have Learnt

观看介绍在路由器中进行操作的视频，把命令和中文连线。
Watch the video introducing the operations in the router, and connect the commands with the Chinese.

① 创建目录 (create directory)   A. cd

② 修改用户当前的工作目录 (modify the user's current working directory)   B. mkdir

③ 查看当前目录下的信息 (check the information in the current directory)   C. rmdir

④ 删除目录 (delete directory)   D. dir

五、小知识 xiǎo zhīshi Tips

dir 命令输出的结果

```
<Huawei>dir
Directory of flash:/src/

  Idx  Attr     Size(Byte)  Date        Time      FileName
    0  -rw-            772  Jun 25 2021 20:49:55  patchfile.src
    1  -rw-            772  Jun 25 2021 20:49:55  patchfilenext.src
    2  drw-              -  Jun 25 2021 21:17:31  niit

32,004 KB total (31,964 KB free)
```

"flash:"表示外部存储器是 flash，"flash:/src/"表示"flash:"的子目录 src。"Idx"表示文件或目录的索引（或称为序号）。"Attr"表示属性，"Attr"分为四部分：第一部分表示文件或目录，"d"表示的是目录，"-"表示的是文件；后面三部分表示权限，"r"表示可读，"w"表示可写，"x"表示可执行。"Size (Byte)"表示文件的大小。"Date"表示日期。"Time"表示时间。"FileName"表示文件名或目录名。

Output Result of the dir Command

"flash:" indicates that the external memory is flash, and "flash:/src/" indicates the subdirectory src of "flash:". "Idx" indicates the index (or serial number) of a file or directory.

"Attr" indicates attribute. "Attr" is divided into four parts: the first part indicates file or directory, with "d" indicating directory and "-"indicating file; the last three parts indicate permissions, with "r" indicating readable, "w" indicating writable, and "x" indicating executable. "Size (Byte)" indicates the file size, "Date" indicates the date, "Time" indicates the time, and "FileName" indicates the file or directory name.

补充专业词语 bǔchōng zhuānyè cíyǔ Supplementary Specialized Vocabulary 🎧 05-07

外部存储器	wàibù cúnchǔqì	phr.	external memory
外部	wàibù	n.	outside
存储器	cúnchǔqì	n.	memory

第二部分 Part 2 汉字 Chinese Characters

一、汉字知识 Hànzì zhīshi Knowledge about Chinese Characters

1. 汉字的笔画（5） **Strokes of Chinese characters (5)**

笔画 Strokes	名称 Names	例字 Examples
乀	斜钩 xiégōu	我
乚	卧钩 wògōu	心
𠃍	横折钩 héngzhégōu	问
乙	横折弯钩 héngzhéwāngōu	几

2. 汉字的结构（1） **Structures of Chinese characters (1)**

结构类型 Structure type	例字 Examples	结构图示 Illustration
独体结构 Independent structure	生 不	☐

62

二、汉字认读与书写　Hànzì rèndú yǔ shūxiě　The Recognition and Writing of Chinese Characters

认读下列汉字构成的词语，并试着写汉字。
Read the words composed of the following Chinese characters, and try to write them.

文件系统　　创建　　删除　　修改　　复制　　显示目录

文			件			系			统		
创			建			删			除		
修			改			复			制		
显			示			目			录		

第三部分　Part 3

日常用语　Daily Expressions

❶ 我要两张 11 号到上海的火车票。Wǒ yào liǎng zhāng 11 hào dào Shànghǎi de huǒchēpiào.
I need two train tickets to Shanghai on the 11th.

❷ 我的护照和钱包都丢了。Wǒ de hùzhào hé qiánbāo dōu diū le. I've lost my passport and wallet.

❸ 还可以便宜一些吗？Hái kěyǐ piányi yìxiē ma? Can you make it cheaper?

第四部分　Part 4

单元实训　Unit Practical Training

目录和文件命令　Directory and File Commands

实训目的　Training purpose

掌握交换机、路由器的目录和文件操作命令的使用。
To master the use of directory and file operation commands of switches and routers.

实训组织 Training organization

每组 3～5 人，选出一个组长。

Students work in groups of 3-5. Each group chooses a group leader.

实训内容 Training content

使用交换机进行目录的 dir、mkdir、rmdir、pwd、cd 命令操作，使用路由器进行文件的 copy、rename、move、delete 命令操作。

Operating the directory commands of dir, mkdir, pwd and cd with the switch, and operating the file commands of copy, rename, move and delete with the router.

实训步骤 Training steps

❶ 将参加实训的人员分成若干小组，每组 3～5 人，轮流上机操作与实践。训练每位同学对知识的掌握程度及操作的熟练程度。

Divide the students into groups of 3-5. Group members take turns to operate and practice on the computer to train each student's mastery of knowledge and proficiency in operation.

❷ 宣布比赛规则及要求：每组每人可以多次操作，安排专人记录每位同学操作所花费的时间，其他组同学监督。

Announce the competition rules and requirements: Each group member can operate for many times. A student is specially assigned to record the time each student takes to operate, with the students of other groups supervising.

❸ 开始比赛。

Start the competition.

1）目录命令操作

directory command operation

启动交换机，按以下顺序输入命令：

Start the switch and enter the commands in the following order:

cd src

mkdir mydir

rmdir mydir

pwd

dir

2）文件命令操作

file command operation

启动路由器，按以下顺序输入命令：

Start the router and enter the commands in the following order:

copy portalpage.zip test.zip

rename test.zip newtest.zip

move newtest.zip dhcp

❹ 计算每组同学总共花费的时间及得分。

Calculate the total time spent and score of each group.

❺ 实训结束，总结评价。
The teacher makes a summary and an evaluation, and ends the training.

第五部分　Part 5　单元小结　Unit Summary

词语 cíyǔ Vocabulary

普通词语　General Vocabulary

1.	主要	zhǔyào	adj.	main
2.	指定	zhǐdìng	v.	specify
3.	其他	qítā	pron.	other
4.	才	cái	adv.	used to indicate that sth. happens only on certain conditions
5.	以	yǐ	prep.	by, with
6.	例	lì	n.	example
7.	记住	jìzhù	phr.	remember

专业词语　Specialized Vocabulary

1.	目录	mùlù	n.	directory
2.	显示	xiǎnshì	v.	display
3.	删除	shānchú	v.	delete
4.	文件	wénjiàn	n.	file
5.	复制	fùzhì	v.	copy
6.	重命名	chóng mìng//míng	phr.	rename
	重	chóng	adv.	again
	命名	mìng//míng	v.	name
7.	移动	yídòng	v.	move
8.	启动	qǐdòng	v.	start
9.	交换机	jiāohuànjī	n.	switch

补充专业词语　Supplementary Specialized Vocabulary

	外部存储器	wàibù cúnchǔqì	phr.	external memory
	外部	wàibù	n.	outside
	存储器	cúnchǔqì	n.	memory

jùzi **句子** Sentences	1. 目录命令主要有显示目录、创建目录、删除目录、显示当前路径、进入指定目录。 2. 文件命令主要有复制文件、重命名文件、移动文件、删除文件。 3. 显示文件和目录信息用 dir 命令。 4. 创建一个 student 的目录，用 \<Huawei\>mkdir student 命令。 5. 把目录删除，用 rmdir 命令。如果提示是否删除，输入 y 即可删除。 6. 显示当前路径，用 pwd 命令。

6 配置文件管理
Configuration File Management

查看配置和处理文件系统异常情况的操作及命令
Operations and Commands for Checking the Configuration and Handling File System Abnormalities

```
<Huawei>display current-configuration
#
sysname Huawei
......
#
Return
```

用 display current-configuration 命令，查看当前配置

<Huawei> display current-configuration

Check the current configuration with the "display current-configuration" command: <Huawei>display current-configuration.

```
fixdisk flash:
Fixdisk flash: may take some time to complete...
%Fixdisk flash: completed.
```

当存储设备的文件系统出现异常时，可以用 fixdisk 命令修复

<Huawei>fixdisk flash:

When the file system in the storage turns to be abnormal, it can be fixed with the "fixdisk" command: <Huawei>fixdisk flash:.

```
<Huawei>display saved-configuration
#
sysname Huawei
......
#
Return
```

用 display saved-configuration 命令，查看保存的配置文件

<Huawei> display saved-configuration

Check the configuration file saved with the "display saved-configuration" command: <Huawei>display saved-configuration.

```
format flash:
All data on flash: will be lost, proceed with format? [Y/N]:y
./
%Format flash: completed.
```

存储设备格式化。格式化会导致数据丢失。

<Huawei> format flash:

Format the storage. Formatting will cause data loss: <Huawei>format flash:

67

题解　Introduction

1. 学习内容：将内存里的命令以文件形式保存在磁盘中的操作方法及配置文件管理的方法。
   Learning content: The operation method of saving the commands in the RAM as files into the disk, and the method of configuration file management.
2. 知识目标：掌握配置文件管理中的核心动词，学习汉字的笔画"㇆、㇉"和品字形结构，学写相关汉字。
   Knowledge objectives: To master the core verbs used in the configuration file management, learn the strokes "㇆，㇉" and the 品-shaped structure of Chinese characters, and write the related characters.
3. 技能目标：学会保存和查看配置文件，掌握 save、display、reboot 命令的使用。
   Skill objective: To learn to save and check the configuration file, and master the use of the save, display and reboot commands.

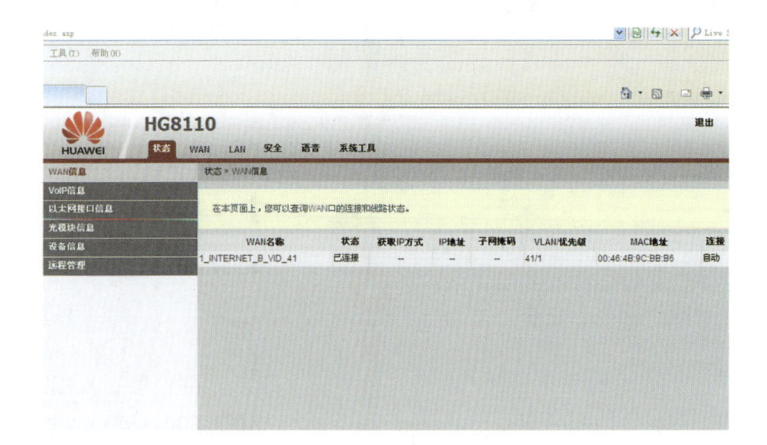

第一部分　Part 1

课文　Texts

一、热身　rèshēn　Warm-up

1. 下列所给的是与配置文件相关的图示，请给词语选择对应的图片。
   The following are illustrations related to configuration file. Please choose the corresponding pictures for the words.

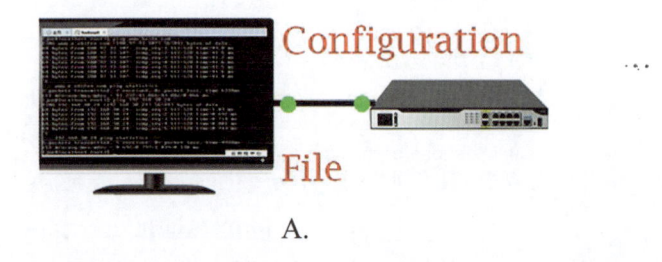

A.　　　　　　　　　　　　　　　　B.

68

配置文件管理
Configuration File Management   6

```
<Huawei>reboot
```
C.

D.

```
<Huawei>display saved-configuration
```
E.

```
<Huawei>startup saved-configuration
```
F.

bǎocún
❶ 保存_____
save

pèizhì wénjiàn
❷ 配置文件_____
configuration file

cúnchǔqì
❸ 存储器_____
memory

chákàn pèizhì wénjiàn
❹ 查看配置文件_____
check configuration file

huīfù pèizhì wénjiàn
❺ 恢复配置文件_____
restore configuration file

chóngqǐ
❻ 重启_____
reboot

2. 观看介绍配置文件的信息的视频，将是否保存了当前配置的图片填在相应的横线上。
Watch the video introducing the information of the configuration file, and fill in the blanks with the pictures of saving or not saving the current configuration.

pèizhì wénjiàn de xìnxī
配置文件的信息
Information of Configuration File

中文+计算机网络技术（中级）

```
┌─────────────────┐      bǎocún        ┌─────────────────┐
│    Current-     │       保存          │     Saved-      │
│Configuration File│ ─────save────▶     │Configuration File│
└─────────────────┘                    └─────────────────┘

┌─────────────────┐      jiāzài        ┌─────────────────┐
│    nèicún       │       加载          │  Flash/SD  kǎ   │
│    内存         │ ◀────load──────    │   Flash/SD 卡    │
│    RAM          │                    │  Flash/SD card  │
└─────────────────┘                    └─────────────────┘
```

A. B. C.

D. E. F.

　　bǎocún dāngqián pèizhì
❶ 保存 当 前 配置 _____
　saving the current configuration

　　wèi bǎocún dāngqián pèizhì
❷ 未 保存 当 前 配置 _____
　not saving the current configuration

二、课文　kèwén　Texts

A 06-01

túdì: Yòng save mìnglìng kěyǐ zuò shénme?
徒弟：用 save 命令可以做什么？

shīfu: Kěyǐ jiāng shèbèi nèicún zhōng de pèizhì xìnxī yǐ wénjiàn xíngshì bǎocún zài shèbèi de cúnchǔqì zhōng, wénjiàn de kuòzhǎnmíng wéi "*.cfg" huò "*.zip".
师傅：可以将设备内存中的配置信息以文件形式保存在设备的存储器中，文件的扩展名为"*.cfg"或"*.zip"。

túdì: Display mìnglìng ne?
徒弟：Display 命令呢？

shīfu: Chákàn shèbèi de pèizhì wénjiàn nèiróng.
师傅：查看设备的配置文件内容。

túdì: Chóngqǐ yòng shénme mìnglìng?
徒弟：重启用什么命令？

shīfu: Yòng reboot.
师傅：用 reboot。

译文 yìwén Text in English

Apprentice: What can I do with the save command?
Master: You can save the configuration information in the device RAM as a file with the extension "*.cfg" or "*.zip".
Apprentice: How about the display command?
Master: It can be used to check the configuration file of the device.
Apprentice: What command is used to restart the device?
Master: Use reboot.

普通词语 pǔtōng cíyǔ General Vocabulary 06-02

1.	将	jiāng	prep.	used to introduce the object before the verb
2.	内存	nèicún	n.	RAM
3.	形式	xíngshì	n.	form

专业词语 zhuānyè cíyǔ Specialized Vocabulary 06-03

1.	配置信息	pèizhì xìnxī	phr.	configuration information
2.	扩展名	kuòzhǎnmíng	phr.	extension
	扩展	kuòzhǎn	v.	extend
	名	míng	n.	name
3.	重启	chóngqǐ	phr.	restart

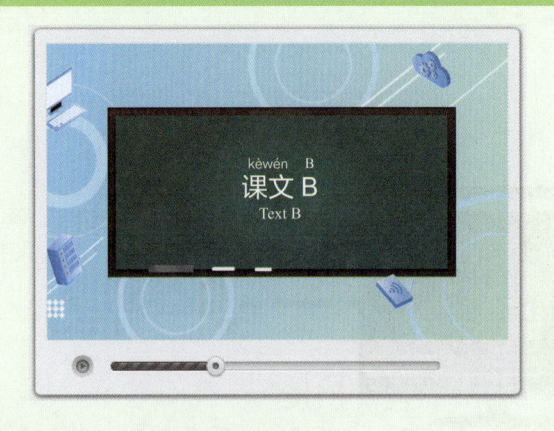

B 06-04

徒弟：配置文件保存在什么地方？
túdì: Pèizhì wénjiàn bǎocún zài shénme dìfang?

师傅：保存在设备的外部存储器的根目录下，外部存储器如 Flash 卡、SD 卡。
shīfu: Bǎocún zài shèbèi de wàibù cúnchǔqì de gēnmùlù xià, wàibù cúnchǔqì rú Flash kǎ、SD kǎ.

6 配置文件管理
Configuration File Management

徒弟：túdì: Rúhé bǎocún pèizhì wénjiàn?
徒弟：如何保存配置文件？

师傅：shīfu: Kěyǐ shǒudòng bǎocún pèizhì wénjiàn, yùnxíng save mìnglìng suíshí bǎocún.
师傅：可以手动保存配置文件，运行save命令随时保存。

徒弟：túdì: Rúguǒ xīwàng zài méi shénme rén shǐyòng jiāohuànjī de shíhou ràng jiāohuànjī chóngqǐ,
徒弟：如果希望在没什么人使用交换机的时候让交换机重启，

kěyǐ ma?
可以吗？

师傅：shīfu: Kěyǐ, bǐrú ràng jiāohuànjī zài wǎnshang 11 diǎn chóngxīn qǐdòng, yòng mìnglìng
师傅：可以，比如让交换机在晚上11点重新启动，用命令

\<Huawei\> schedule reboot at 23:00.
\<Huawei\> schedule reboot at 23:00。

\<Huawei\>display saved-configuration

译文 yìwén Text in English

Apprentice: Where is the configuration file saved?

Master: It is saved in the root directory of the external memory of the device. External memory includes Flash card, SD card, etc.

Apprentice: How to save the configuration file?

Master: You can manually save the configuration file, and run the save command to save it at any time.

Apprentice: Can I reboot the switch when no one is using it?

Master: Yes, you can. For example, reboot the switch at 23:00 with the command < Huawei > schedule reboot at 23:00.

普通词语 pǔtōng cíyǔ General Vocabulary 🎧 06-05

1.	地方	dìfang	n.	place
2.	随时	suíshí	adv.	at any time
3.	希望	xīwàng	v.	hope
4.	没	méi	v.	not have
5.	人	rén	n.	people
6.	让	ràng	v.	let, make

| 7. | 晚上 | wǎnshang | n. | night |
| 8. | 重新 | chóngxīn | adv. | again |

专业词语 zhuānyè cíyǔ Specialized Vocabulary   06-06

| 1. | 根目录 | gēnmùlù | phr. | root directory |
| 2. | 手动 | shǒudòng | adj. | manual |

三、视听说 shì-tīng-shuō Viewing, Listening and Speaking

1. 观看介绍配置文件的视频，并进行连线。
Watch the video introducing the configuration file, and connect the applicable options.

① cóng cúnchǔqì huīfù pèizhì wénjiàn
从 存储器恢复配置文件
recover the configuration file from the memory

A. set save-configuration interval

② běndì zìdòng bǎocún pèizhì wénjiàn
本地自动 保存配置文件
automatically save the configuration file locally

B. *.zip 或 *.cfg

C. startup saved-configuration

③ wénjiàn de kuòzhǎnmíng
文件的 扩展名
file extension

2. 说一说 Let's talk.

说一说如何设置间隔 60 分钟使系统在本地自动保存配置文件。
Talk about how to set the system to automatically save the configuration file locally at 60-minute interval.

四、学以致用 xuéyǐzhìyòng Practicing What You Have Learnt

观看介绍查看配置和处理文件系统异常情况的视频,并把正确选项填在相应横线上。
Watch the video about checking the configuration and handling the file system abnormalities, and fill in the blanks with the right options.

format		display		fixdisk
A.		B.		C.

Chákàn pèizhì wénjiàn de mìnglìng shì:
❶ 查看配置文件的命令是:＿＿＿＿＿
The command to check the configuration file is:

Xiūfù cúnchǔ shèbèi wénjiàn xìtǒng de mìnglìng shì:
❷ 修复存储设备文件系统的命令是:＿＿＿＿＿
The command to fix the file system of the storage device is:

五、小知识 xiǎo zhīshi Tips

Cúnchǔ shèbèi
存储设备

Cúnchǔ shèbèi bāokuò SDRAM、Flash kǎ、NVRAM、SD kǎ、U pán. Lìrú,
存储设备包括SDRAM、Flash卡、NVRAM、SD卡、U盘。例如,

AR2200E de lùyóuqì yǒu nèizhì de shǎncún. Gāi lùyóuqì tígōngle liǎng gè yùliú USB
AR2200E的路由器有内置的闪存。该路由器提供了两个预留USB

chācáo (usb0 hé usb1) hé yí gè SD kǎ chācáo (sd0). S5720 jiāohuànjī bāohán yí gè
插槽(usb0和usb1)和一个SD卡插槽(sd0)。S5720交换机包含一个

nèizhì shǎncún, shǎncún xínghào bù tóng, cúnchǔ róngliàng yě bù tóng, S5720-EI zhīchí 340M
内置闪存,闪存型号不同,存储容量也不同,S5720-EI支持340M

shǎncún, S5720-HI zhīchí 400M shǎncún.
闪存,S5720-HI支持400M闪存。

> **Storage Devices**
>
> The storage devices include SDRAM, Flash card, NVRAM, SD card and USB flash drive. For example, the AR2200E router has a built-in flash memory. The router provides two reserved USB slots (usb0 and usb1) and one SD card slot (sd0). S5720 switch contains a built-in flash memory, which has different storage capacity for different models. S5720-EI supports 340M flash memory, and S5720-HI supports 400M flash memory.

补充专业词语 bǔchōng zhuānyè cíyǔ Supplementary Specialized Vocabulary 🎧 06-07

| 插槽 | chācáo | n. | slot |

第二部分 Part 2 汉字 Chinese Characters

一、汉字知识 Hànzì zhīshi Knowledge about Chinese Characters

1. 汉字的笔画（6） Strokes of Chinese characters (6)

笔画 Strokes	名称 Names	例字 Examples
㇇	横撇弯钩 héngpiěwāngōu	部
㇠	横折折折钩 héngzhézhézhégōu	奶

2. 汉字的结构（2） Structures of Chinese characters (2)

结构类型 Structure type	例字 Example	结构图示 Illustration
品字形结构 品-shaped structure	品	⯊

配置文件管理 6
Configuration File Management

二、汉字认读与书写　Hànzì rèndú yǔ shūxiě　The Recognition and Writing of Chinese Characters

认读下列汉字构成的词语，并试着写汉字。

Read the words composed of the following Chinese characters, and try to write them.

保存命令　　配置文件　　存储器　　重启设备　　根目录

保				存				命				令			
配				置				文				件			
存				储				器				重			
启				设				备				根			
目				录											

第三部分　Part 3　日常用语　Daily Expressions

① 请原谅。Qǐng yuánliàng. Pardon me, please./ Forgive me, please.
② 不好意思，麻烦你……Bù hǎoyìsi, máfan nǐ…… Excuse me, could you please...
③ 我前几天感冒了。Wǒ qián jǐ tiān gǎnmào le. I had a cold several days ago.

第四部分　Part 4　单元实训　Unit Practical Training

pèizhì wénjiàn de cāozuò
配置文件的操作
Operations on Configuration File

配置文件的操作 Operations on Configuration File

实训目的 Training purpose
掌握 save、display、reboot 命令的使用，培养团队合作精神、竞争意识。

To master the use of save, display and reboot commands, and cultivate spirit of teamwork and competitive consciousness.

实训组织 Training organization
每组 3～5 人，选出一个组长。

Students work in groups of 3-5. Each group chooses a group leader.

实训内容 Training content
保存、查看配置文件。

Saving and checking the configuration file.

实训步骤 Training steps

❶ 按小组轮流上机操作与实践。训练每位同学对知识的掌握程度及操作的熟练程度。

Groups take turns to operate and practice on the computer to train each student's mastery of knowledge and proficiency in operations.

❷ 宣布比赛规则及要求：每组每人可以多次上机操作，安排专人记录每位同学操作所花费的时间，其他组同学监督。

Announce the competition rules and requirements: Each group member can operate on the computer for many times. A student is specially assigned to record the time each student takes to operate, with the students of other groups supervising.

❸ 开始比赛。

Start the competition.

1）运行 eNSP 软件，新建拓扑。

Run the eNSP software to create a new topology.

2）选择 S3700 交换机，启动交换机。

Select S3700 switch and start it.

3）保存配置文件。

Save the configuration file.

① 手动保存。<Huawei>save

Save manually. <Huawei>save

② 自动保存。<Huawei>system-view [Huawei]set save-configuration interval 60

Save automatically. <Huawei>system-view[Huawei]set save-configuration interval 60

③ 保存为文件。<Huawei>save config.cfg

Save as file. <Huawei>save config.cfg

4）重启交换机。<Huawei>reboot

Restart the switch. <Huawei>reboot

5）查看命令。

Check the commands.

① 查看设备版本信息。<Huawei>display version

Check the device version information. <Huawei>display version

② 查看当前配置。<Huawei>display current-configuration

Check the current configuration. <Huawei>display current-configuration

③ 查看配置文件。<Huawei>display saved-configuration

Check the configuration file. <Huawei>display saved-configuration

④ 计算每组同学总共花费的时间及得分。

Calculate the total time spent and score of each group.

⑤ 实训结束，总结评价。

The teacher makes a summary and an evaluation, and ends the training.

第五部分 Part 5 单元小结 Unit Summary

词语 Vocabulary

普通词语 General Vocabulary

1.	将	jiāng	prep.	*used to introduce the object before the verb*
2.	内存	nèicún	n.	RAM
3.	形式	xíngshì	n.	form
4.	地方	dìfang	n.	place
5.	随时	suíshí	adv.	at any time
6.	希望	xīwàng	v.	hope
7.	没	méi	v.	not have
8.	人	rén	n.	people
9.	让	ràng	v.	let, make
10.	晚上	wǎnshang	n.	night
11.	重新	chóngxīn	adv.	again

专业词语 Specialized Vocabulary

1.	配置信息	pèizhì xìnxī	phr.	configuration information
2.	扩展名	kuòzhǎnmíng	phr.	extension
	扩展	kuòzhǎn	v.	extend
	名	míng	n.	name
3.	重启	chóngqǐ	phr.	restart

cíyǔ 词语 Vocabulary	4.	根目录	gēnmùlù	phr.	root directory
	5.	手动	shǒudòng	adj.	manual
	补充专业词语　Supplementary Specialized Vocabulary				
		插槽	chācáo	n.	slot
jùzi 句子 Sentences	1. 用 save 命令可以将设备内存中的配置信息以文件形式保存在设备的存储器中。 2. 配置文件保存在设备的外部存储器的根目录下。 3. 可以手动保存配置文件，运行 save 命令随时保存。 4. 可以让交换机在晚上 11 点重新启动。				

7

Xūnǐ juyùwǎng
虚拟局域网
Virtual Local Area Network

zài yì tái jiāohuànjī shang huàfēn liǎng gè VLAN de pèizhì guòchéng
在一台 交换机 上 划分 两 个 VLAN 的配置 过程
Configuration Process of Dividing 2 VLANs on a Switch

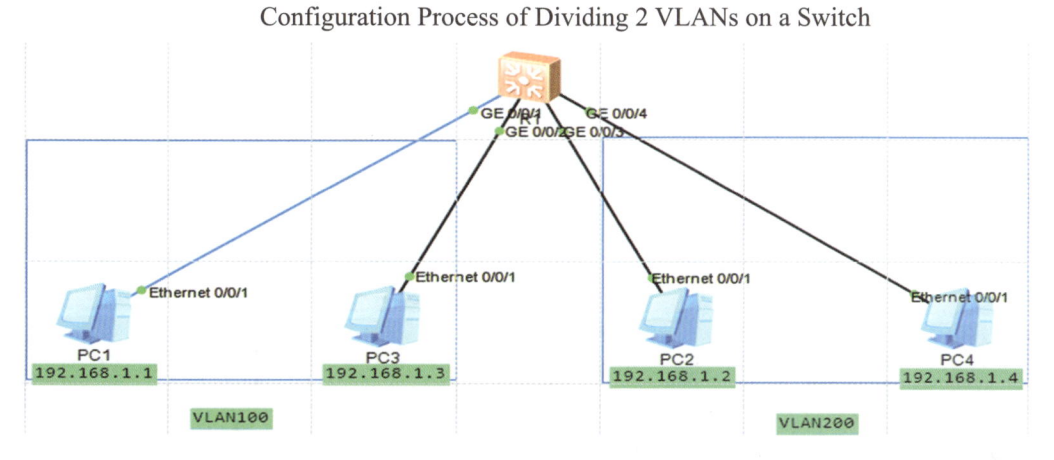

dāntái jiāohuànjī jiē 4 tái diànnǎo
1. 单台 交换机 接 4 台 电脑

   Four computers are connected to a single switch.

   pèizhì liǎng gè xūnǐ zǐwǎng: VLAN 100 hé VLAN 200,
2. 配置 两 个虚拟子网：VLAN 100 和 VLAN 200，
   PC1 hé PC3 shǔyú VLAN 100, PC2 hé PC4 shǔyú
   PC1 和 PC3 属于 VLAN 100，PC2 和 PC4 属于
   VLAN 200, chákàn PC jiān de liántōng qíngkuàng, yànzhèng
   VLAN 200，查看 PC 间的 连通 情况， 验证
   VLAN huàfēn qíngkuàng.
   VLAN 划分 情况 。

   Configure two virtual subnets: VLAN100 and VLAN200.
   PC1 and PC3 belong to VLAN 100, and PC2 and PC4 belong to VLAN 200. Check the connectivity between PCs to verify the VLAN division.

   PC1 hé PC3 xiānghù néng Ping tōng, PC3 hé PC4 xiānghù néng
3. PC1 和 PC3 相互 能 Ping 通，PC3 和 PC4 相互 能
   Ping tōng, yīnwèi tāmen zài tóng yí gè zǐwǎng. PC2 hé PC3
   Ping 通，因为 它们 在 同一个 子网。PC2 和 PC3
   xiānghù bù néng Ping tōng, yīnwèi tāmen bú zài tóng yí gè zǐwǎng.
   相互 不 能 Ping通，因为 它们不在 同 一个 子网。

   PC1 and PC3 can ping each other, and PC3 and PC4 can ping each other because they are in the same subnet, but PC2 and PC3 cannot ping each other because they are not in the same subnet.

81

> **题解　Introduction**
>
> 1. 学习内容：虚拟局域网的创建及划分 VLAN 的作用。
>   Learning content: The creation of virtual local area network and the functions of dividing the VLAN.
> 2. 知识目标：掌握创建 VLAN 关键步骤的核心动词，学习汉字的笔画"㇆、乀"和结构"上下结构、上中下结构"，学写相关汉字
>   Knowledge objectives: To master the core verbs used in the key steps when creating the VLAN, learn the strokes "㇆、乀", the top-bottom structure and the top-middle-bottom structure of Chinese characters, and write the related characters.
> 3. 技能目标：根据公司的实际需求，创建虚拟局域网。
>   Skill objective: To create the VLAN according to the company's practical needs.

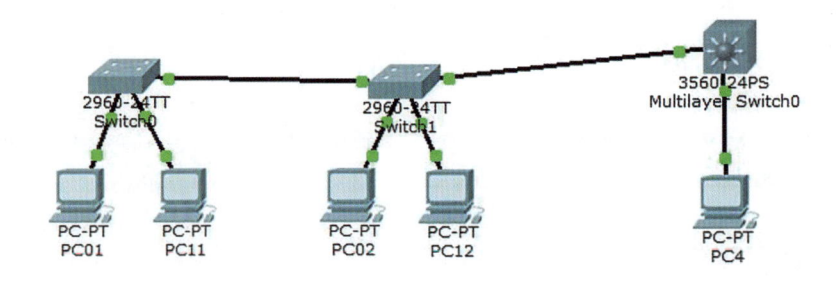

第一部分　Part 1

课文　Texts

一、热身　rèshēn　Warm-up

1. 关于虚拟局域网的优点，请选出你认为正确的选项。
   Choose the options you think are right regarding the advantages of VLAN.

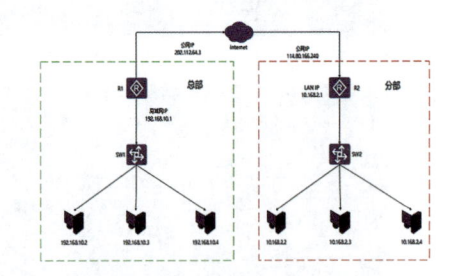

   A. 提高异地间的互通
   tígāo yìdì jiān de hùtōng
   improving the connectivity between different places

   B. 提高带宽利用率
   tígāo dàikuān lìyònglǜ
   increasing the use ratio of the bandwidth

虚拟局域网
Virtual Local Area Network

C. 不受物理位置影响
bú shòu wùlǐ wèizhi yǐngxiǎng
not affected by physical locations

D. 分组自由
fēn zǔ zìyóu
grouping freedom

E. 增强局域网的安全性
zēngqiáng júyùwǎng de ānquánxìng
enhancing the security of LAN

F. 提供建立防火墙机制
tígōng jiànlì fánghuǒqiáng jīzhì
providing firewall creating mechanism

关于虚拟局域网的优点，你认为正确的选项是：_____
Guānyú xūnǐ júyùwǎng de yōudiǎn, nǐ rènwéi zhèngquè de xuǎnxiàng shì:
About the advantages of VLAN, the right options that you think are:

2. 观看介绍虚拟局域网的特点和功能的视频，将正确的选项填在横线上。
   Watch the video introducing the characteristics and functions of VLAN, and fill in the blanks with the right options.

虚拟局域网的特点和功能
xūnǐ júyùwǎng de tèdiǎn hé gōngnéng
Characteristics and Functions of VLAN

83

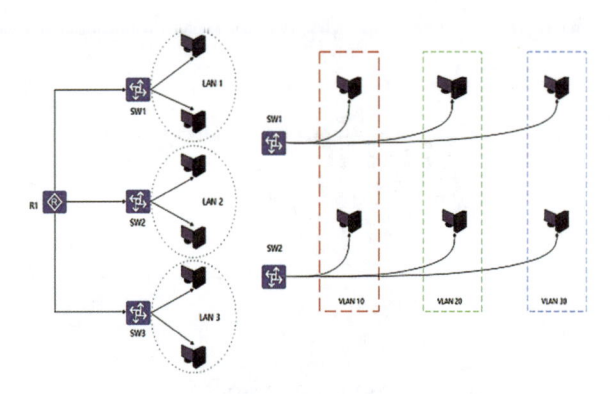

shì yì zǔ luóji shang de shèbèi hé yònghù
A. 是一组逻辑上的设备和用户
it's a set of logical devices and users

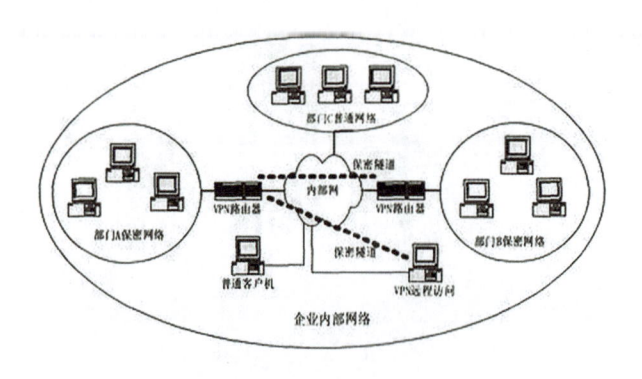

bāngzhù shíxiàn fǎngwèn kòngzhì gōngnéng
B. 帮助实现访问控制功能
it helps realize access control functions

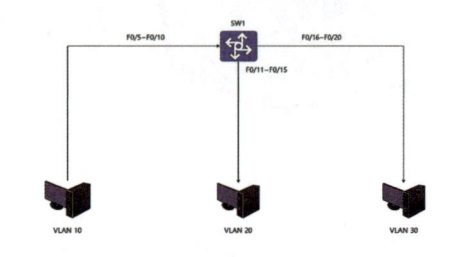

bāngzhù shíxiàn xìnxī xìtǒng wú rǎo gòngxiǎng
C. 帮助实现信息系统无扰共享
it helps realize undisturbed sharing of information systems

néng jiǎnshǎo guǎnlǐ kāixiāo
D. 能减少管理开销
it can reduce management cost

tígāo wǎngluò de ānquánxìng
E. 提高网络的安全性
it improves the security of network

shǐ LAN gèng jù línghuóxìng
F. 使 LAN 更具灵活性
it makes LAN more flexible

Guānyú xūnǐ júyùwǎng de tèdiǎn hé gōngnéng, zhèngquè de xuǎnxiàng shì:
关于虚拟局域网的特点和功能，正确的选项是：＿＿＿＿＿＿
About the characteristics and functions of VLAN, the right options are:

7 虚拟局域网
Virtual Local Area Network

二、课文 kèwén Texts

A 07-01

课文 A
Text A

túdì: Shénme shì VLAN?
徒弟：什么 是 VLAN？

shīfu: VLAN shì Yīngwén Virtual Local Area Network de jiǎnchēng, yòu jiào xūnǐ
师傅：VLAN 是 英文 Virtual Local Area Network 的 简称，又叫 虚拟

júyùwǎng.
局域网。

túdì: Zhè shì yì zhǒng shénme jìshù?
徒弟：这 是 一种 什么 技术？

shīfu: Shì tōngguò jiāng júyùwǎng nèi de shèbèi cóng luóji shang huàfēn wéi yí gègè wǎngduàn,
师傅：是 通过 将 局域网 内 的 设备 从 逻辑 上 划分 为一个个 网段，

cóng'ér shíxiàn xūnǐ gōngzuòzǔ de jìshù.
从而实现虚拟工作组的技术。

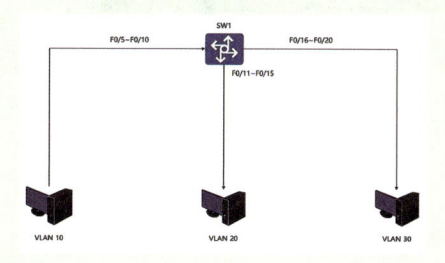

译文 yìwén Text in English

Apprentice: What is a VLAN?
Master: VLAN is the abbreviation of Virtual Local Area Network, also known as virtual LAN.
Apprentice: What kind of technology is it?
Master: It is a technology that realizes the virtual working group by logically dividing the devices in the LAN into network segments.

普通词语 pǔtōng cíyǔ General Vocabulary 🎧 07-02

1.	英文	Yīngwén	pn.	English
2.	简称	jiǎnchēng	n.	abbreviation
3.	又	yòu	adv.	also
4.	叫	jiào	v.	be called
5.	内	nèi	n.	inside
6.	划分	huàfēn	v.	divide
7.	从而	cóng'ér	conj.	thus, thereby

专业词语 zhuānyè cíyǔ Specialized Vocabulary 🎧 07-03

1.	VLAN			Virtual Local Area Network
2.	虚拟	xūnǐ	adj.	virtual
3.	技术	jìshù	n.	technology
4.	逻辑	luóji	n.	logic
5.	网段	wǎngduàn	n.	network segment
6.	工作组	gōngzuòzǔ	n.	working group

B 🎧 07-04

课文 B
Text B

túdì: Shīfu, qǐngwèn VLAN yǒu jǐ zhǒng lèixíng?
徒弟：师傅，请问 VLAN 有几种 类型？

shīfu: Gēnjù huàfēn yuánzé de bù tóng, VLAN zhǔyào fēnwéi sān lèi.
师傅：根据划分原则的不同，VLAN 主要分为三类。

túdì: Qǐngwèn jùtǐ shì nǎ sān lèi ne?
徒弟：请问 具体是哪三类呢？

shīfu: Jīyú duānkǒu de VLAN、 jīyú MAC dìzhǐ de VLAN hé jīyú xiéyì
师傅：基于端口的 VLAN、基于 MAC 地址的 VLAN 和基于协议
de VLAN.
的 VLAN。

túdì:	Nàme nǎ yì zhǒng VLAN yùnyòng zuì guǎng ne?	
徒弟：	那么哪一种VLAN 运用 最 广 呢？	
shīfu:	Jīyú duānkǒu de VLAN zài shíjì de wǎngluò yìngyòng zhōng zuìwéi guǎngfàn.	
师傅：	基于 端口 的VLAN在实际的网络 应用 中 最为 广泛。	

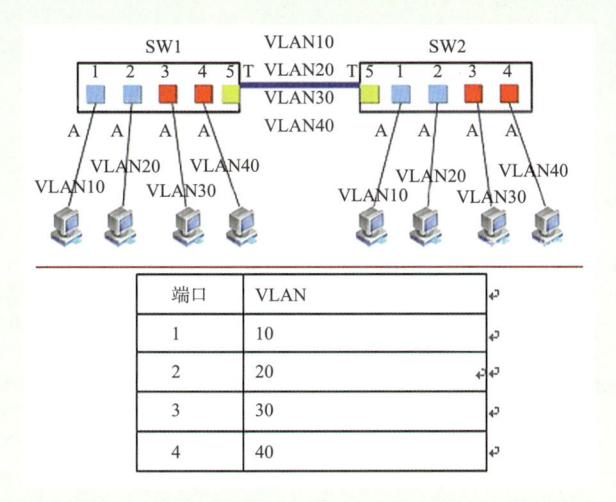

端口	VLAN
1	10
2	20
3	30
4	40

译文 yìwén Text in English

Apprentice: Master, how many types of VLANs are there?

Master: According to different division principles, VLANs are mainly divided into three types.

Apprentice: May I ask what the three types are?

Master: Port-based VLANs, MAC address-based VLANs and protocol-based VLANs.

Apprentice: Then which type of VLAN is the most widely used?

Master: Port-based VLANs are the most widely used in practical network applications.

普通词语 pǔtōng cíyǔ General Vocabulary 07-05

1.	根据	gēnjù	prep.	according to
2.	原则	yuánzé	n.	principle
3.	类	lèi	m.	type, kind
4.	具体	jùtǐ	adj.	specific
5.	那么	nàme	conj.	then
6.	运用	yùnyòng	v.	use
7.	最	zuì	adv.	most
8.	广	guǎng	adj.	wide
9.	实际	shíjì	adj.	practical
10.	应用	yìngyòng	v.	apply
11.	最为	zuìwéi	adv.	most

| 12. | 广泛 | guǎngfàn | adj. | wide |

专业词语 zhuānyè cíyǔ Specialized Vocabulary 🎧 07-06

1.	基于	jīyú	prep.	on account of
2.	端口	duānkǒu	n.	port
3.	MAC 地址	MAC dìzhǐ	phr.	Media Access Control address
	地址	dìzhǐ	n.	address
4.	协议	xiéyì	n.	protocol

三、视听说 shì-tīng-shuō Viewing, Listening and Speaking

1. 观看介绍电脑间的连通情况的视频，并把正确答案填在横线上。
Watch the video introducing the connectivity between computers, and fill in the blanks with the right answers.

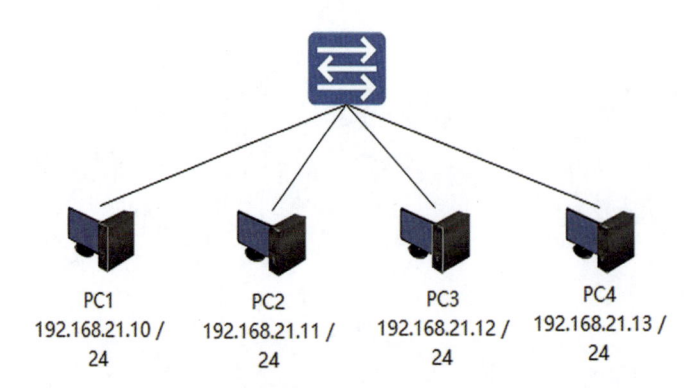

单台交换机接4台电脑不划分 VLAN 时电脑间的连通情况
dāntái jiāohuànjī jiē 4 tái diànnǎo bù huàfēn VLAN shí diànnǎo jiān de liántōng qíngkuàng
Connectivity Between Computers When a Single Switch is Connected to 4 Computers and VLAN is not Divided

PC1 192.168.21.10 / 24
PC2 192.168.21.11 / 24
PC3 192.168.21.12 / 24
PC4 192.168.21.13 / 24

Shìpín zhōng de shíyàn jiéguǒ xiǎnshì: Bú huàfēn VLAN shí, PC1、PC2、PC3 hé PC4 shì:
视频中的实验结果显示：不划分 VLAN 时，PC1、PC2、PC3 和 PC4 是：_____。

The result of the experiment in the video shows that when VLAN is not divided, PC1, PC2, PC3 and PC4 are:

2. 说一说 Let's talk.

说一说划分 VLAN 时，在同一个子网和不在同一个子网的电脑间的连通性有什么不同。

Talk about the differences in connectivity between computers in the same subnet and computers not in the same subnet when VLAN is divided.

四、学以致用 xuéyǐzhìyòng Practicing What You Have Learnt

观看介绍在一台交换机上划分两个 VLAN 的配置过程的视频。划分 VLAN 后，PC1 和 PC3 在一个虚拟子网中，PC2 和 PC4 在另一个虚拟子网中。根据问题在表中相应位置打"√"：

Watch the video introducing the configuration process of dividing two VLANs on a switch. When the division is finished, PC1 and PC3 are in one virtual subnet, and PC2 and PC4 are in another virtual subnet. Tick in the corresponding boxes in the table according to the questions.

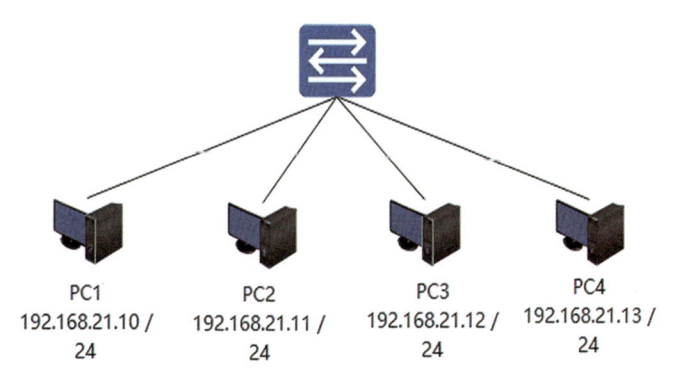

PC1 192.168.21.10 / 24   PC2 192.168.21.11 / 24   PC3 192.168.21.12 / 24   PC4 192.168.21.13 / 24

❶ PC1、PC3 可以互相 Ping 通吗？为什么？
Can PC1 and PC3 ping each other? Why?

❷ PC2、PC3 可以互相 Ping 通吗？为什么？
Can PC2 and PC3 ping each other? Why?

❸ PC1、PC4 可以互相 Ping 通吗？为什么？
Can PC1 and PC4 ping each other? Why?

wèntí 问题 Questions	PCs	liántōng xìng 连通性 Connectivity		yuányīn 原因 Reason	
		Yes	No	zài tóng yí gè zǐwǎng A. 在同一个子网 They are in the same subnet.	bú zài tóng yí gè zǐwǎng B. 不在同一个子网 They are not in the same subnet.
1	PC1 & PC3				
2	PC2 & PC3				
3	PC1 & PC4				

五、小知识　xiǎo zhīshi　Tips

Huàfēn VLAN de zuòyòng
划分 VLAN 的作用

VLAN shì wèi jiějué yǐtàiwǎng de guǎngbō wèntí hé ānquánxìng ér tíchū de, yí gè
VLAN 是为解决以太网的广播问题和安全性而提出的，一个
VLAN nèibù de guǎngbō hé dānbō liúliàng dōu bú huì zhuǎnfā dào qítā VLAN zhōng. Jíshǐ
VLAN 内部的广播和单播流量都不会转发到其他 VLAN 中。即使
shì chǔzài tóng yí gè wǎngduàn de liǎng tái jìsuànjī, rúguǒ bú zài tóngyī VLAN zhōng, tāmen
是处在同一个网段的两台计算机，如果不在同一 VLAN 中，它们
gèzì de guǎngbōliú yě bú huì hùxiāng zhuǎnfā.
各自的广播流也不会互相转发。

Functions of the Division of VLAN

VLAN is created to solve the broadcast problem and security of the Ethernet. The broadcast and unicast traffic within a VLAN will not be forwarded to other VLANs. Even for the two computers in the same network segment, if thcy are not in the same VLAN, their respective broadcast streams will not be forwarded to each other.

补充专业词语　bǔchōng zhuānyè cíyǔ　Supplementary Specialized Vocabulary　🎧 07-07

1. 广播流　　guǎngbōliú　　　phr.　　broadcast stream
2. 流量　　　liúliàng　　　　　n.　　　traffic, flow

第二部分　Part 2　汉字　Chinese Characters

一、汉字知识　Hànzì zhīshi　Knowledge about Chinese Characters

1. 汉字的笔画（7）Strokes of Chinese characters (7)

笔画 Strokes	名称 Names	例字 Examples
㇉	竖折折钩 shùzhézhégōu	马
㇟	横折斜钩 héngzhéxiégōu	风

2. 汉字的结构（3）Structures of Chinese characters (3)

结构类型 Structure type	例字 Examples	结构图示 Illustrations
上下结构 Top-bottom structure	爸 节	日 日
上中下结构 Top-middle-bottom structure	意	三

二、汉字认读与书写　Hànzì rèndú yǔ shūxiě　The Recognition and Writing of Chinese Characters

认读下列汉字构成的词语，并试着写汉字。
Read the words composed of the following Chinese characters, and try to write them.

虚拟局域网　相通　子网　逻辑　技术

虚		拟		局		域	
网		相		通		子	
网		逻		辑		技	
术							

第三部分　Part 3

日常用语　Daily Expressions

① 麻烦你替我请个假。Máfan nǐ tì wǒ qǐng gè jiǎ. Would you please ask for leave for me?

② 我被骗了。Wǒ bèi piàn le. I was cheated.

③ 别着急。Bié zháojí. Don't worry.

第四部分　Part 4

单元实训　Unit Practical Training

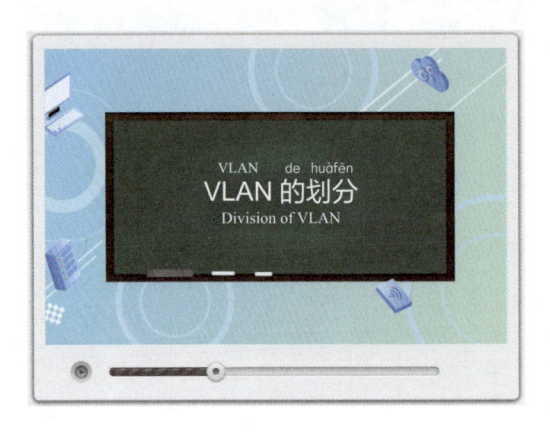

VLAN 的划分　Division of VLAN

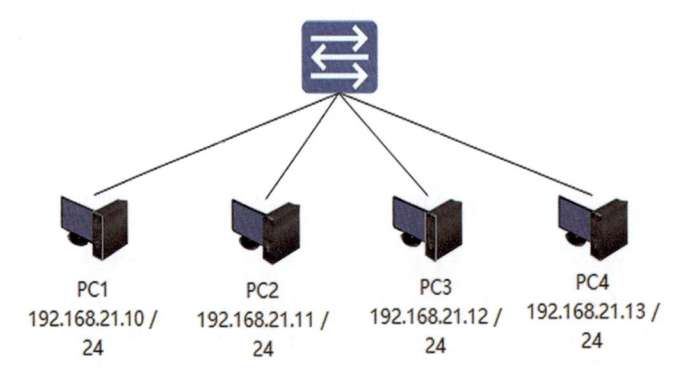

PC1　PC2　PC3　PC4
192.168.21.10 / 24　192.168.21.11 / 24　192.168.21.12 / 24　192.168.21.13 / 24

某公司的交换网络如上图所示，其中 PC1 和 PC3 同属于一个部门，PC2 和 PC4 同属于另一个部门。为了阻断不同部门之间的二层通信，需要划分两个 VLAN，分别为 VLAN 100、VLAN 200。

The above diagram shows the switching network of a company. PC1 and PC3 belong to one department, and PC2 and PC4 belong to another. To block Layer 2 communication between different departments, the company needs to divide two VLANs — VLAN 100 and VLAN 200.

实训目的　Training purpose

掌握在交换机上创建 VLAN 的步骤，并实现相关配置，验证 VLAN 划分的效果。

To master the steps of creating VLAN on the switch, realize relevant configuration, and verify the effect of VLAN division.

实训组织 Training organization

每组 3～5 人，选出一个组长。

Students work in groups of 3-5. Each group chooses a group leader.

实训内容 Training content

根据公司网络拓扑及其他具体情况，通过配置指令实现基于端口的 VLAN 划分，并对 VLAN 划分前后的效果进行验证。

According to the company's network topology and other specific situations, realize the port-based VLAN division through configuration instructions, and verify the effect before and after dividing VLAN.

实训步骤 Training steps

❶ 在交换机上创建 VLAN。

Create VLAN on the switch.

❷ 配置交换机上连接 PC 的端口为 Access 模式，并加入相应的 VLAN。

Configure the port connecting PC on the switch to Access mode, and include it in corresponding VLAN.

❸ 测试不同 PC 间的连通性，验证 VLAN 划分的效果。

Test the connectivity between different PCs to verify the effect of VLAN division.

❹ 实训结束，总结评价。

The teacher makes a summary and an evaluation, and ends the training.

第五部分　Part 5　单元小结　Unit Summary

词语 cíyǔ Vocabulary

普通词语　General Vocabulary

1.	英文	Yīngwén	pn.	English
2.	简称	jiǎnchēng	n.	abbreviation
3.	又	yòu	adv.	also
4.	叫	jiào	v.	be called
5.	内	nèi	n.	inside
6.	划分	huàfēn	v.	divide
7.	从而	cóng'ér	conj.	thus, thereby
8.	根据	gēnjù	prep.	according to
9.	原则	yuánzé	n.	principle
10.	类	lèi	m.	type, kind
11.	具体	jùtǐ	adj.	specific
12.	那么	nàme	conj.	then

cíyǔ 词语 Vocabulary

13.	运用	yùnyòng	v.	use
14.	最	zuì	adv.	most
15.	广	guǎng	adj.	wide
16.	实际	shíjì	adj.	practical
17.	应用	yìngyòng	v.	apply
18.	最为	zuìwéi	adv.	most
19.	广泛	guǎngfàn	adj.	wide

专业词语 Specialized Vocabulary

1.	VLAN			Virtual Local Area Network
2.	虚拟	xūnǐ	adj.	virtual
3.	技术	jìshù	n.	technology
4.	逻辑	luóji	n.	logic
5.	网段	wǎngduàn	n.	network segment
6.	工作组	gōngzuòzǔ	n.	working group
7.	基于	jīyú	prep.	on account of
8.	端口	duānkǒu	n.	port
9.	MAC 地址	MAC dìzhǐ	phr.	Media Access Control address
	地址	dìzhǐ	n.	address
10.	协议	xiéyì	n.	protocol

补充专业词语 Supplementary Specialized Vocabulary

| 1. | 广播流 | guǎngbōliú | phr. | broadcast stream |
| 2. | 流量 | liúliàng | n. | traffic, flow |

jùzi 句子 Sentences

1. VLAN 又叫虚拟局域网，是通过将局域网内的设备从逻辑上划分为一个个网段，从而实现虚拟工作组的技术。
2. 根据划分原则的不同，VLAN 主要分为三类：基于端口的 VLAN、基于 MAC 地址的 VLAN 和基于协议的 VLAN。
3. 基于端口的 VLAN 在实际的网络应用中最为广泛。

8 IP 地址与子网掩码
IP Address and Subnet Mask

IP 地址所在网络的网络地址计算过程
Calculation Process of Network Address Where the IP Address is Located

将一个子网掩码与一个IP地址进行逐位"与"运算,所得的结果便是该IP地址所在网络的网络地址。看下面这个例子:

Perform a bitwise "AND" operation between a subnet mask and an IP address, and the result is the address of the network where the IP address is located. Look at the following example:

	第一字节 First byte	第二字节 Second byte	第三字节 Third byte	第四字节 Fourth byte
IP 地址 IP address	11010010	00011100	01100100	00001010
子网掩码 Subnet mask	11111111	11111111	11111111	00000000
逐位相"与"运算结果 Result of bitwise "AND" operation	11010010	00011100	01100100	00000000
网络地址 Network address	210	28	100	0

> **题解　Introduction**
>
> 1. 学习内容：IP 地址、子网掩码及其结合使用的含义，IP 地址所在网络的网络地址的计算过程。
>   Learning content: The meaning of IP address, subnet mask and the combined use of them two, and the calculation process of the network address where the IP address is located.
> 2. 知识目标：掌握 IP 地址与子网掩码结合使用中的核心词语，学习汉字的笔画"丶、乁"和"左右结构、左中右结构"，学写相关汉字。
>   Knowledge objectives: To master the core vocabulary used in the combined use of IP address and subnet mask, learn the strokes "丶, 乁", the left-right structure and the left-middle-right structure of Chinese characters, and write the related characters.
> 3. 技能目标：配置 IP 地址并验证连通性。
>   Skill objective: To configure IP address and verify the connectivity.

IP 地址和子网掩码计算所在网段

	131	107	41	6
二进制地址	10000011	01101011	00101001	00000110
与	255	255	255	0
二进制子网掩码	11111111	11111111	11111111	00000000
	131	107	41	0
地址和子网掩码做"与"运算得到网络号	10000011	01101011	00101001	00000000

地址 131.107.41.6　子网掩码 255.255.255.0

第一部分　Part 1

课文　Texts

一、热身　rèshēn　Warm-up

1. 判断下列图片哪些是子网掩码。 Judge which of the following pictures are subnet masks.

11111111 11111111 11111111 11111111 （255.255.255.255）

A.

00000000 00000000 00000000 00000000 （0.0.0.0）

B.

11011000 00000000 00000000 00000000 （216.0.0.0）

C.

00000000 11111111 11111111 11111111 （0.255.255.255）

D.

11111100 00000000 00000000 00000000 （252.0.0.0）

E.

11111111 11111111 11111111 11110000 （255.255.255.240）

F.

Shì zǐwǎng yǎnmǎ de túpiàn wéi:
是 子网 掩码 的 图片 为：_____。
The pictures of subnet masks are:

2. 观看介绍子网掩码长度的视频，将下列子网掩码与其对应的长度连线。

Watch the video introducing the length of subnet masks, and connect the following subnet masks to the corresponding lengths.

❶ 255.255.0.0　　　　　　　　　　　　　　　A. 8 位

❷ 255.255.255.0　　　　　　　　　　　　　　B. 28 位

❸ 255.0.0.0　　　　　　　　　　　　　　　　C. 24 位

❹ 255.255.255.240　　　　　　　　　　　　　D. 16 位

二、课文　kèwén　Texts

A 08-01

徒弟：师傅，什么是 IP 地址？

师傅：IP 地址是用来标识 TCP/IP 网络中每台主机或设备的一个地址，由两部分组成。

徒弟：哪两部分？

师傅：左边为网络地址，用网络编号来标识主机所在的网络，即"网络号"；右边为主机地址，用来标识主机本身，即"主机号"。

因特网部分	本地部分
网络号 net-id	主机号 host-id

IP 地址

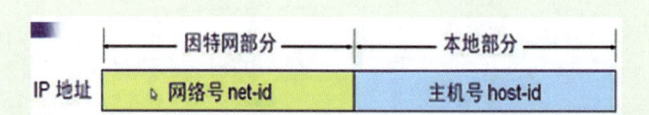

译文 yìwén Text in English

Apprentice: Master, what is the IP address?

Master: The IP address is the address used to identify each host or device in TCP/IP network. It consists of two parts.

Apprentice: Which two parts?

Master: On the left is the network address with the network number identifying the network where the host is located, i.e. the net ID. On the right is the host address which is used to identify the host itself, i.e. the host ID.

普通词语 pǔtōng cíyǔ General Vocabulary 🎧 08-02

1.	标识	biāoshí	v.	identify, indicate
2.	左边	zuǒbian	n.	left
3.	即	jí	adv.	i.e., namely
4.	右边	yòubian	n.	right
5.	本身	běnshēn	pron.	oneself

专业词语 zhuānyè cíyǔ Specialized Vocabulary 🎧 08-03

1.	TCP/IP 网络	TCP/IP wǎngluò	phr.	TCP/IP network
2.	网络号	wǎngluòhào	phr.	net ID
3.	主机号	zhǔjīhào	phr.	host ID

B 🎧 08-04

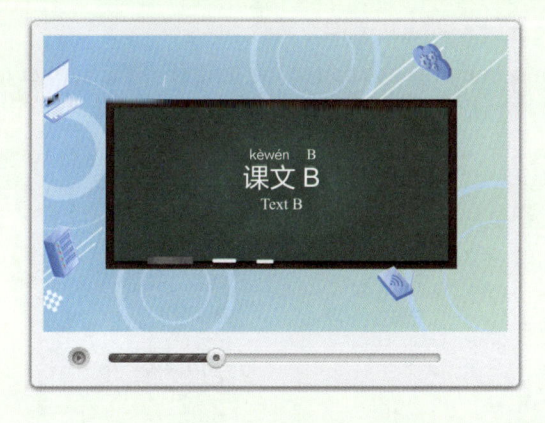

课文 B
Text B

师傅：子网掩码由32个比特组成，通常以点分十进制数来表示。

徒弟：子网掩码用二进制表示时，是由1和0组成的，对吗？

师傅：子网掩码由若干个连续的1后接若干个连续的0组成，或者由32个0或32个1组成。

徒弟：子网掩码的长度如何计算？

shīfu: Tōngcháng jiāng yí gè zǐwǎng yǎnmǎ zhōng 1 de gèshù chēngwéi zhège zǐwǎng yǎnmǎ de
师傅：通常　　将一个子网　掩码　中　1的个数　称为　这个子网　掩码的

chángdù.
长度。

子网掩码（十进制表示）	子网掩码（二进制表示）	子网掩码长度
255.255.255.0	11111111.11111111.11111111.00000000	24

译文 yìwén Text in English

Master: A subnet mask consists of 32 bits and is usually represented in dotted decimal numbers.
Apprentice: A subnet mask is made up of 1 and 0 when it is represented in binary system, right?
Master: A subnet mask is composed of a number of consecutive 1s followed by a number of consecutive 0s, or is composed of 32 0s or 32 1s.
Apprentice: How to calculate the length of a subnet mask?
Master: Usually the number of 1s in a subnet mask is called the length of the subnet mask.

普通词语 pǔtōng cíyǔ General Vocabulary   🎧 08-05

1.	通常	tōngcháng	adv.	usually
2.	数	shù	n.	number
3.	表示	biǎoshì	v.	indicate, show
4.	对	duì	adj.	right
5.	若干	ruògān	pron.	a number of, several
6.	连续	liánxù	v.	go on uninterruptedly
7.	后接	hòu jiē	phr.	be followed by
	接	jiē	v.	follow
8.	或者	huòzhě	conj.	or
9.	长度	chángdù	n.	length
10.	计算	jìsuàn	v.	calculate
11.	个数	gèshù	phr.	number

专业词语 zhuānyè cíyǔ Specialized Vocabulary   🎧 08-06

1.	比特	bǐtè	n.	bit
2.	点分十进制	diǎnfēn shíjìnzhì	phr.	dotted decimal notation
3.	二进制	èrjìnzhì	phr.	binary system

三、视听说　shì-tīng-shuō　Viewing, Listening and Speaking

1. 观看介绍网络地址计算过程的视频，根据给出的 IP 地址和子网掩码，以及此 IP 地址所在网络的网络地址 210.28.100.0，理解计算过程并选择填空。

Watch the video introducing the calculation process of the network address. Understand the calculation process, and fill in the blanks with right choices according to the given IP address and subnet mask and the network address 210.28.100.0 where the IP address is located.

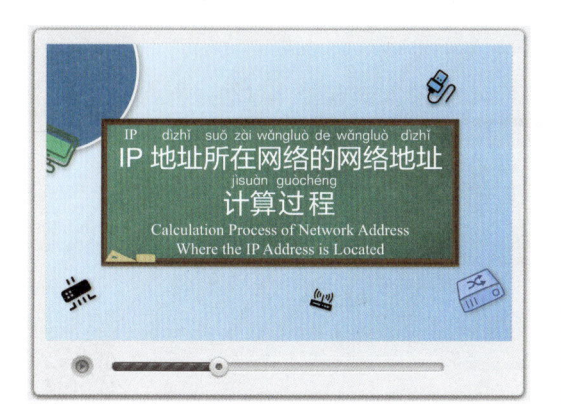

	dì-yī zìjié 第一字节 First byte	dì-èr zìjié 第二字节 Second byte	dì-sān zìjié 第三字节 Third byte	dì-sì zìjié 第四字节 Fourth byte
IP dìzhǐ IP 地址 IP address	11010010	00011100	01100100	00001010
zǐwǎng yǎnmǎ 子网掩码 Subnet mask	11111111	11111111	01100100	00000000
zhú wèi xiāng "yǔ" yùnsuàn jiéguǒ 逐位相"与"运算结果 Result of bitwise "AND" operation	❶_____	❷_____	❸_____	❹_____
wǎngluò dìzhǐ 网络地址 Network address	210	28	100	0

A. 11010010　　　B. 00011100　　　C. 01100100　　　D. 00000000

2. 说一说　Let's talk.

说一说 IP 地址所在网络的网络地址计算过程。

Talk about the calculation process of the network address where the IP address is located.

四、学以致用 xuéyǐzhìyòng Practicing What You Have Learnt

观看视频,根据下列计算过程填空,并判断这两个 IP 地址所在网络的网络地址是否相同,以及它们是否在同一个子网内。

Watch the video, fill in the blanks according to the following calculation process, and judge whether the network addresses where the two IP addresses are located are the same and whether they are in the same subnet.

IP dìzhǐ 1: 192.168.21.10/24
IP 地址 1:192.168.21.10/24
IP address 1: 192.168.21.10/24

	dì-yī zìjié 第一字节 First byte	dì-èr zìjié 第二字节 Second byte	dì-sān zìjié 第三字节 Third byte	dì-sì zìjié 第四字节 Fourth byte
IP dìzhǐ IP 地址 IP address	11000000	10101000	00010101	00001010
zǐwǎng yǎnmǎ 子网掩码 Subnet mask	11111111	11111111	11111111	00000000
zhú wèi xiāng "yǔ" 逐位相"与" yùnsuàn jiéguǒ 运算结果 Result of bitwise "AND" operation	11000000	①_____	②_____	00000000
wǎngluò dìzhǐ 网络地址 Network address	192	168	21	③_____

IP 地址与子网掩码
IP Address and Subnet Mask

IP 地址 2：192.168.21.20/24
IP address 2: 192.168.21.20/24

	第一字节 First byte	第二字节 Second byte	第三字节 Third byte	第四字节 Fourth byte
IP 地址 IP address	11000000	10101000	00010101	00010100
子网掩码 Subnet mask	11111111	11111111	11111111	00000000
逐位相"与"运算结果 Result of bitwise "AND" operation	④_____	10101000	00010101	⑤_____
网络地址 Network address	192	⑥_____	21	0

五、小知识 Tips

子网掩码的表示方式

每个IP地址都有一个与其对应的子网掩码，在书写IP地址及其对应的子网掩码时，习惯IP地址在前，子网掩码在后，中间以"/"隔开；为了方便起见，还常常以子网掩码的长度来代替子网掩码本身。例如，192.168.21.11/255.255.255.0 或 192.168.21.11/24。

Representation Method of Subnet Masks

Each IP address has a corresponding subnet mask. When writing an IP address and its corresponding subnet mask, the IP address usually precedes the subnet mask, with a slash "/" in between to separate them. For the sake of simplicity, the length of the subnet mask is often used to take the place of the subnet mask itself. For example, 192.168.21.11/255.255.255.0 or 192.168.21.11/24.

补充专业词语 bǔchōng zhuānyè cíyǔ Supplementary Specialized Vocabulary   08-07

1.	逐位	zhú wèi	phr.	bitwise
2.	相"与"运算	xiāng "yǔ" yùnsuàn	phr.	"AND" operation
	运算	yùnsuàn	v.	operate, calculate

第二部分 Part 2

汉字 Chinese Characters

一、汉字知识 Hànzì zhīshi Knowledge about Chinese Characters

1. 汉字的笔画（8） Strokes of Chinese characters (8)

笔画 Strokes	名称 Names	例字 Examples
ㄥ	竖弯 shùwān	四
ㄟ	横折弯 héngzhéwān	没

2. 汉字结构（4） Structures of Chinese characters (4)

结构类型 Structure types	例字 Examples	结构图示 Illustrations
左右结构 Left-right structure	银 饭	▯▯
左中右结构 Left-middle-right structure	班 微	▯▯▯

二、汉字认读与书写 Hànzì rèndú yǔ shūxiě The Recognition and Writing of Chinese Characters

认读下列汉字构成的词语，并试着写汉字。

Read the words composed of the following Chinese characters, and try to write them.

子网掩码　　比特　　计算　　存储器

子 网 掩 码
比 特 计 算
存 储 器

104

IP 地址与子网掩码
IP Address and Subnet Mask

第三部分 Part 3 — 日常用语 Daily Expressions

1. 你不能这样。Nǐ bù néng zhèyàng. You can't be like that.
2. 我马上就到。Wǒ mǎshàng jiù dào. I will be there right away.
3. 让我想想。Ràng wǒ xiǎngxiang. Let me think.

第四部分 Part 4 — 单元实训 Unit Practical Training

配置 IP 地址并验证连通性
Configuring IP Address and Verifying the Connectivity

配置 IP 地址并验证连通性 Configuring IP Address and Verifying the Connectivity

实训目的 Training purpose
掌握 IP 地址配置的步骤，并验证连通性。
To master the steps of configuring the IP address and verify the connectivity.

实训组织 Training organization
每组 4 人，选出一个组长。
Students work in groups of 4. Each group chooses a group leader.

实训内容 Training content
配置 IP 地址，并验证连通性。
Configuring IP addresses and verifying the connectivity.

实训步骤 Training steps

1. 将参加人员分成若干小组，每组 4 人，轮流操作。实验步骤如下面的网络拓扑图所示。
   Divide the students into groups of 4, and the students take turns to operate. The experiment steps are shown in the following network topology diagram.

   1）在路由器 R 的每个端口设置一个 IP；
   Set an IP address for every port of router R;

   2）路由器每个端口接入一台交换机；
   Connect every port of the router to a switch;

105

3）每台交换机接两台 PC，每台 PC 设 IP 地址；
  Connect each switch to two PCs. Assign each PC an IP address;

4）验证连通性。
  Verify the connectivity.

❷ 实验完毕之后，根据小组实验成功人数及完成时间打分。
  After the experiment, mark each group according to the number of group members who have successfully finished the experiment and the time spent.

❸ 实训结束，总结评价。
  The teacher makes a summary and an evaluation, and ends the training.

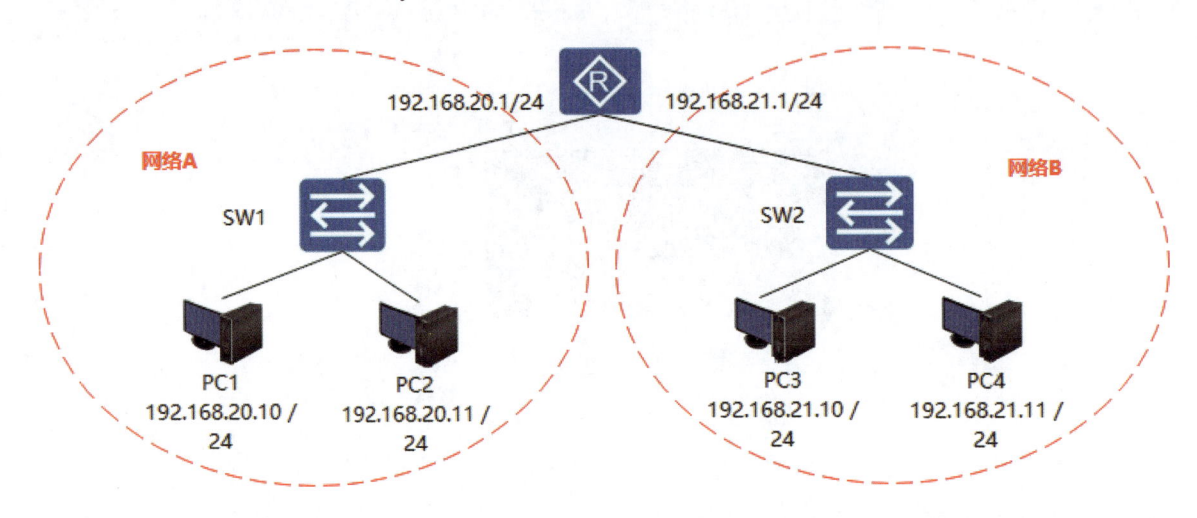

第五部分　Part 5

单元小结　Unit Summary

cíyǔ
词语
Vocabulary

普通词语　General Vocabulary

1.	标识	biāoshí	v.	identify, indicate
2.	左边	zuǒbian	n.	left
3.	即	jí	adv.	i.e., namely
4.	右边	yòubian	n.	right
5.	本身	běnshēn	pron.	oneself
6.	通常	tōngcháng	adv.	usually
7.	数	shù	n.	number
8.	表示	biǎoshì	v.	indicate, show
9.	对	duì	adj.	right
10.	若干	ruògān	pron.	a number of, several
11.	连续	liánxù	v.	go on uninterruptedly

106

IP 地址与子网掩码
IP Address and Subnet Mask

词语 cíyǔ Vocabulary

普通词语 General Vocabulary

12.	后接	hòu jiē	phr.	be followed by
	接	jiē	v.	follow
13.	或者	huòzhě	conj.	or
14.	长度	chángdù	n.	length
15.	计算	jìsuàn	v.	calculate
16.	个数	gèshù	phr.	number

专业词语 Specialized Vocabulary

1.	TCP/IP 网络	TCP/IP wǎngluò	phr.	TCP/IP network
2.	网络号	wǎngluòhào	phr.	net ID
3.	主机号	zhǔjīhào	phr.	host ID
4.	比特	bǐtè	n.	bit
5.	点分十进制	diǎnfēn shíjìnzhì	phr.	dotted decimal notation
6.	二进制	èrjìnzhì	phr.	binary system

补充专业词语 Supplementary Specialized Vocabulary

1.	逐位	zhú wèi	phr.	bitwise
2.	相 "与" 运算	xiāng "yǔ" yùnsuàn	phr.	"AND" operation
	运算	yùnsuàn	v.	operate, calculate

句子 jùzi Sentences

1. IP 地址是用来标识 TCP/IP 网络中每台主机或设备的一个地址。
2. IP 地址由两部分组成。左边为网络地址,用网络编号来标识主机所在的网络,即"网络号";右边为主机地址,用来标识主机本身,即"主机号"。
3. 子网掩码由 32 个比特组成,通常以点分十进制数来表示。
4. 子网掩码由若干个连续的 1 后接若干个连续的 0 组成,或者由 32 个 0 或 32 个 1 组成。
5. 通常将一个子网掩码中 1 的个数称为这个子网掩码的长度。

9 用路由器组建网络
Yòng lùyóuqì zǔjiàn wǎngluò
Constructing a Network with Routers

jìngtài lùyóu pèizhì bùzhòu
静态路由配置 步骤
Steps of Configuring Static Routing

xiàzài bìng ānzhuāng eNSP ruǎnjiàn
下载并 安装 eNSP 软件
download and install the eNSP software

qǐdòng suǒ xū lùyóuqì
启动 所需路由器
start the required router

dǎkāi jìsuànjī mónǐqì, shèzhì IP dìzhǐ, zǐwǎng yǎnmǎ hé wǎngguān
打开计算机模拟器，设置 IP 地址、子网 掩码和 网关
open the computer simulator and set the IP address, subnet mask and gateway

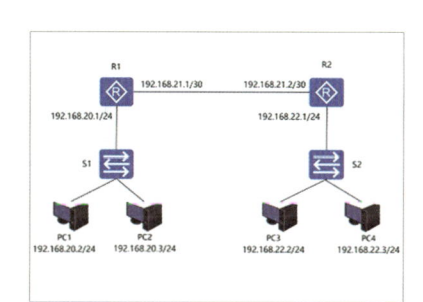

dǎkāi eNSP ruǎnjiàn, huìzhì wǎngluò tuòpūtú
打开 eNSP 软件，绘制 网络 拓扑图
open the eNSP software and draw the network topology diagram

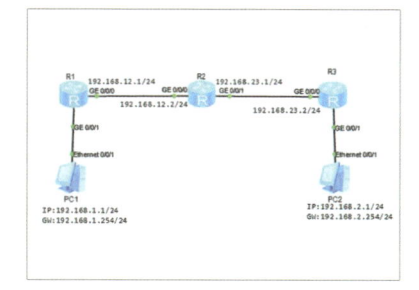

dǎkāi lùyóuqì mónǐqì, jìnxíng jìngtài lùyóu pèizhì
打开路由器模拟器，进行 静态 路由 配置
open the router simulator and perform static routing configuration

bǎocún pèizhì, bìng cèshì jìsuànjī liántōngxìng
保存 配置，并测试计算机 连通性
save the configuration and test the computer connectivity

109

题解　Introduction

1. 学习内容：eNSP 软件上的常用图标含义，以及静态路由配置流程。
   Learning content: The meaning of the common icons on the eNSP software and the configuration process of static routing.

2. 知识目标：掌握静态路由配置流程中关键步骤里的核心动词，学习汉字的笔画 "㇆、乚" 和 "全包围结构、半包围结构"，学写相关汉字。
   Knowledge objectives: To master the core verbs used in the key steps of the static routing configuration process, learn the strokes "㇆、乚", the fully-enclosed structure and the semi-enclosed structure of Chinese characters, and write the related characters.

3. 技能目标：用静态路由配置流程设置 IP 地址，使得 PC1 和 PC3 能相互通信。
   Skill objective: To set the IP address with static routing configuration process to enable the communication between PC1 and PC3.

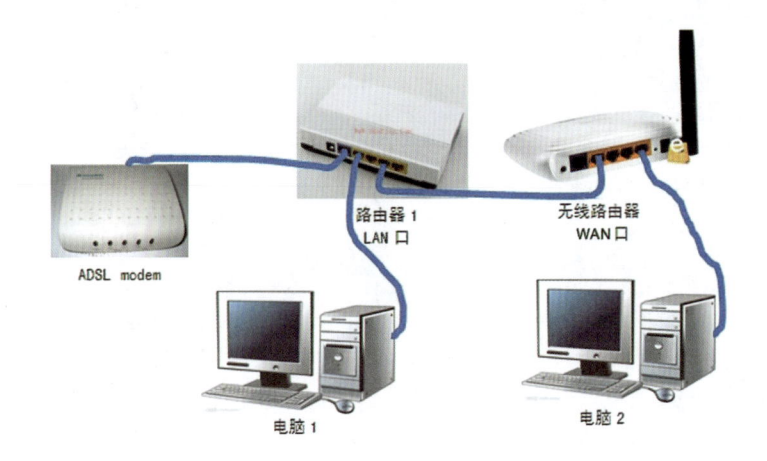

第一部分　Part 1

课文　Texts

一、热身　rèshēn　Warm-up

1. 下列所给的图示是 eNSP 软件上的标识，请给词语选择对应的图示。
The illstrations given below are the icons on the eNSP software. Please choose the corresponding illustrations for the words.

A.　　　　B. AR1　　　　C. LSW1

110

D.   E.   F.

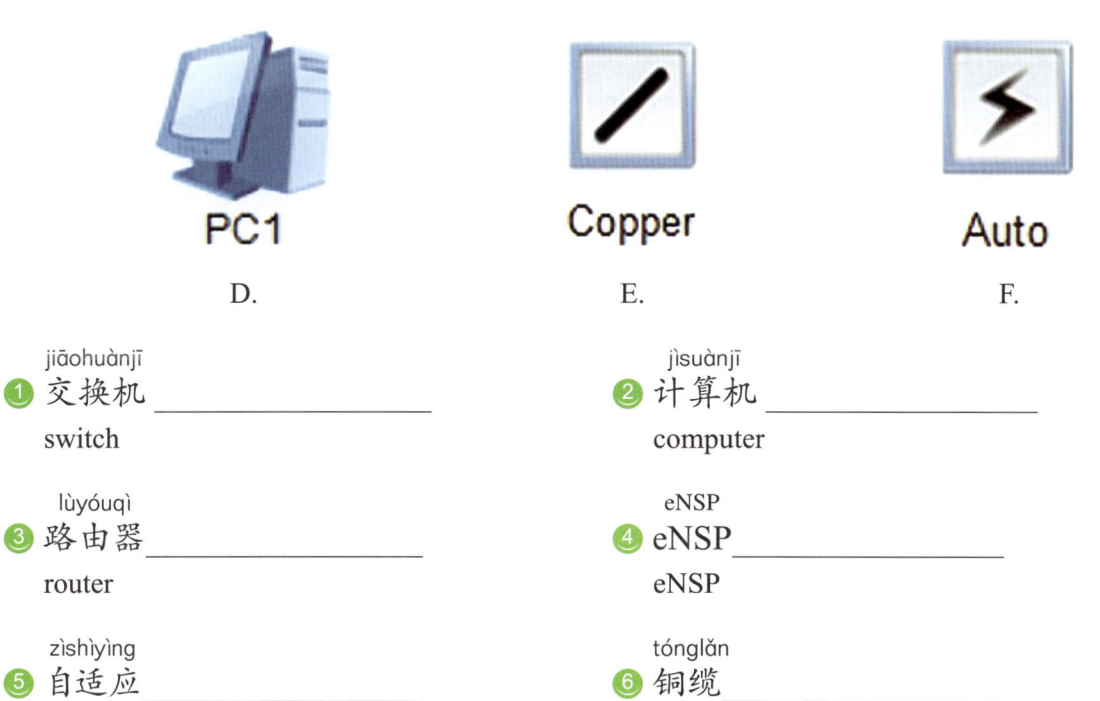

❶ jiāohuànjī
交换机 _____
switch

❷ jìsuànjī
计算机 _____
computer

❸ lùyóuqì
路由器 _____
router

❹ eNSP
eNSP _____
eNSP

❺ zìshìyìng
自适应 _____
self-adaption

❻ tónglǎn
铜缆 _____
copper cable

2. 观看介绍静态路由配置流程的视频，将这些动作与其匹配的内容连线。
Watch the video introducing the process of configuring static routing, and connect these actions to the corresponding contents.

静态路由配置步骤
Steps of Configuring Static Routing

111

① ānzhuāng 安装 install	A. lùyóuqì 路由器 router	
② cèshì 测试 test	B. IP dìzhǐ IP 地址 IP address	
③ huìzhì 绘制 draw	C. eNSP ruǎnjiàn eNSP 软件 eNSP software	
④ qǐdòng 启动 start	D. liántōngxìng 连通性 connectivity	
⑤ shèzhì 设置 set	E. wǎngluò tuòpūtú 网络拓扑图 network topology diagram	

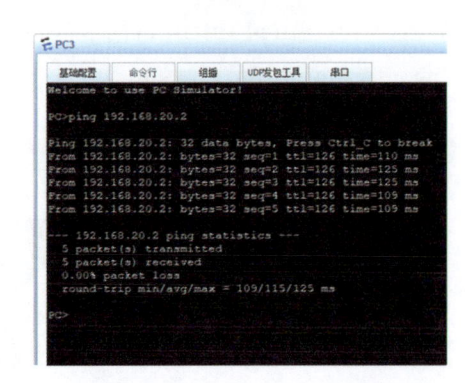

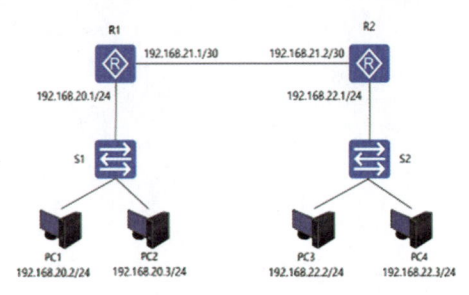

二、课文 kèwén Texts

A 09-01

túdì: Shénme shì jìngtài lùyóu?
徒弟：什么是静态路由？

shīfu: Shǒugōng pèizhì de lùyóu xìnxī chēngwéi jìngtài lùyóu.
师傅：手工配置的路由信息称为静态路由。

túdì: Zài pèizhì jìngtài lùyóu qián xūyào zuò shénme ne?
徒弟：在配置静态路由前需要做什么呢？

shīfu: Wǒmen xūyào ānzhuāng eNSP, ránhòu huìzhì wǎngluò tuòpūtú.
师傅：我们需要安装 eNSP，然后绘制网络拓扑图。

译文 yìwén Text in English

Apprentice: What is static routing?
Master: The routing information configured manually is called static routing.
Apprentice: What do we need to do before configuring a static routing?
Master: We need to install the eNSP and draw a network topology diagram.

专业词语 zhuānyè cíyǔ Specialized Vocabulary 09-02

1.	静态路由	jìngtài lùyóu	phr.	static routing
	静态	jìngtài	adj.	static
	路由	lùyóu	n.	routing
2.	手工配置	shǒugōng pèizhì	phr.	manual configuration
	手工	shǒugōng	n.	handwork
3	路由信息	lùyóu xìnxī	phr.	routing information
4.	eNSP			Enterprise Network Simulation Platform (a network emulator from Huawei)

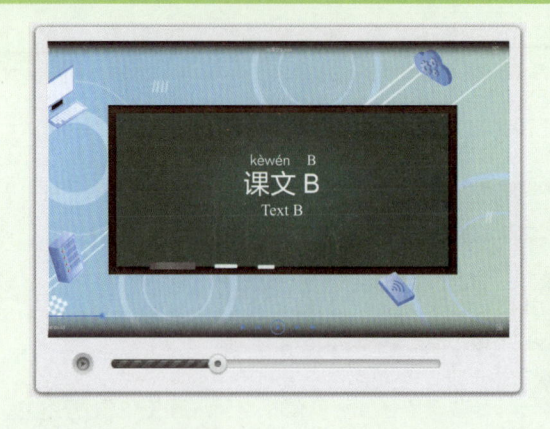

徒弟：静态路由怎么配置呢？

师傅：先在路由器的两个端口配置IP地址，然后进行静态路由配置。

徒弟：那在计算机上要做什么配置呢？

师傅：我们需要配置好IP地址、子网掩码和网关。

徒弟：那我们怎么才能知道配置好了呢？

师傅：我们可以用Display ip routing-table查看配置，然后测试计算机之间的连通性。

译文 yìwén Text in English

Apprentice: How to configure the static routing?

Master: First, configure the IP address on the two ports of the router, and then configure the static routing.

Apprentice: Then what configuration should be done on the computer?

Master: We need to configure the IP address, subnet mask and gateway.

Apprentice: Then how do we know that the configuration is done?

Master: We can use Display ip routing-table to check the configuration, and then test the connectivity between the computers.

用路由器组建网络
Constructing a Network with Routers

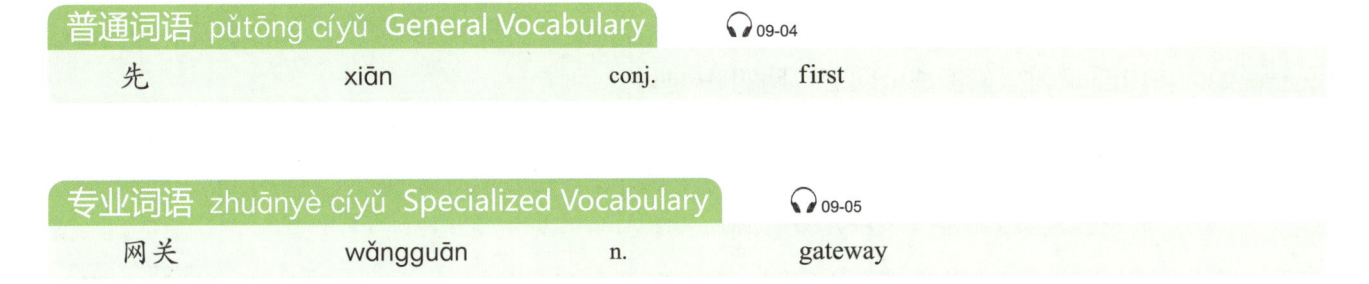

普通词语 pǔtōng cíyǔ General Vocabulary　🎧 09-04

| 先 | xiān | conj. | first |

专业词语 zhuānyè cíyǔ Specialized Vocabulary　🎧 09-05

| 网关 | wǎngguān | n. | gateway |

三、视听说　shì-tīng-shuō　Viewing, Listening and Speaking

1. 观看介绍私有 IP 地址通过 NAT 转换成公有地址的视频，将 A、B、C 三类私有地址与其范围连线。
Watch the video about transforming private IP addresses to public IP addresses via NAT, and connect the three classes of private IP addresses A, B, C to their ranges.

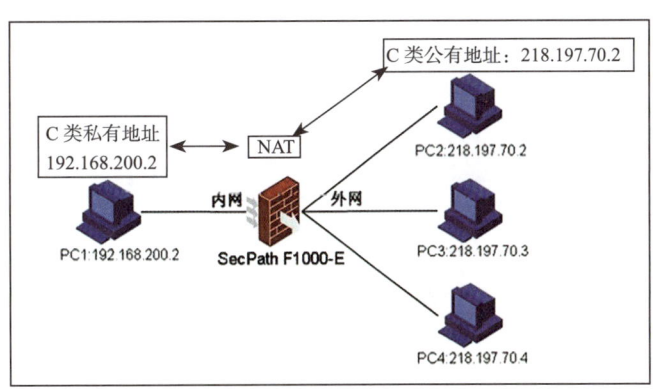

❶ A lèi sīyǒu dìzhǐ
　A 类私有地址　　　　　　　　　　　　A. 192.168.0.0~192.168.255.255
　class A private IP addresses

❷ B lèi sīyǒu dìzhǐ
　B 类私有地址　　　　　　　　　　　　B. 10.0.0.0~10.255.255.255
　class B private IP addresses

❸ C lèi sīyǒu dìzhǐ
　C 类私有地址　　　　　　　　　　　　C. 172.16.0.0~172.31.255.255
　class C private IP addresses

115

2. 说一说　Let's talk.

说一说如何将内部 IP 地址转换成公网上可用的 IP 地址。

Talk about how to transform internal IP addresses into IP addresses available on the public network.

四、学以致用　xuéyǐzhìyòng　Practicing What You Have Learnt

观看视频，了解从 R1 到 R2 静态路由的配置，是如何设置 IP 地址，使得 PC1 和 PC3 能相互通信的，并把四台电脑与其 IP 地址连线。

Watch the video to learn about how the IP address is set in the configuration of static routing from R1 to R2 to enable PC1 and PC3 to communicate with each other, and connect the four computers to their IP addresses.

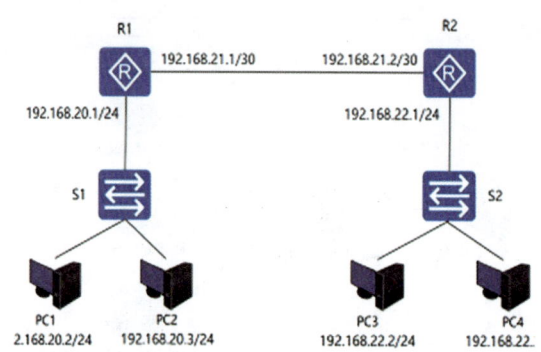

❶ PC1　　　　　　　　　　　　　　A. 192.168.22.3/24

❷ PC2　　　　　　　　　　　　　　B. 192.168.22.2/24

❸ PC3　　　　　　　　　　　　　　C. 192.168.20.2/24

❹ PC4　　　　　　　　　　　　　　D. 192.168.20.3/24

五、小知识　xiǎo zhīshi　Tips

两个子网中的计算机之间如何通信
Liǎng gè zǐwǎng zhōng de jìsuànjī zhījiān rúhé tōngxìn

静态路由用于网段较少、带宽不高的小型网络。它的路由项由手动配置，是固定的：即使网络状况发生改变，它也不会改变。一般来说，静态路由是由网络管理员逐项加入路由表的。配置完静态路由，两个子网中的计算机之间就可以通信了。

How the Computers in Two Subnets Communicate with Each Other

The static routing is used for small networks with fewer network segments and low bandwidth. Its routing entries are configured manually and fixed: it will not change even if the network condition changes. In general, the static routing entries are added to the routing table item by item by the network administrator. When static routing is configured, computers in two subnets can communicate with each other.

补充专业词语　bǔchōng zhuānyè cíyǔ　Supplementary Specialized Vocabulary　09-06

1.	相互通信	xiānghù tōngxìn	phr.	communicate with each other
	相互	xiānghù	adv.	mutually
2.	私有 IP 地址	sīyǒu IP dìzhǐ	phr.	private IP address
	私有	sīyǒu	v.	own privately
3.	NAT			Network Address Translation

第二部分　Part 2
汉字　Chinese Characters

一、汉字知识　Hànzì zhīshi　Knowledge about Chinese Characters

1. 汉字的笔画（9）Strokes of Chinese characters (9)

笔画 Strokes	名称 Names	例字 Examples
㇋	横折折撇 héngzhéhépiě	延、建
ㄣ	竖折撇 shùzhépiě	专

2. 汉字的结构（5） **Character structures (5)**

结构类型 Structure types	例字 Examples	结构图示 Illustrations
全包围结构 Fully-enclosed structure	国	□
半包围结构 Semi-enclosed structure	医 边 问 唐 凶	□ □ □ □ □

二、汉字认读与书写　Hànzì rèndú yǔ shūxiě　**The Recognition and Writing of Chinese Characters**

认读下列汉字构成的词语，并试着写汉字。
Read the words composed of the following Chinese characters, and try to write them.

静态路由　　私有地址　　安装　　配置

静			态			路			由	
私			有			地			址	
安			装			配			置	

第三部分　Part 3　日常用语 *Daily Expressions*

① 我该怎么办？ Wǒ gāi zěnme bàn? What shall I do?
② 麻烦你告诉我他的电话号码。Máfan nǐ gàosu wǒ tā de diànhuà hàomǎ. Excuse me, could you please tell me his phone number?
③ 真不好意思，我忘了给你打电话。Zhēn bù hǎoyìsi, wǒ wàngle gěi nǐ dǎ diànhuà. Sorry, I forgot to phone you.

第四部分　Part 4　单元实训 Unit Practical Training

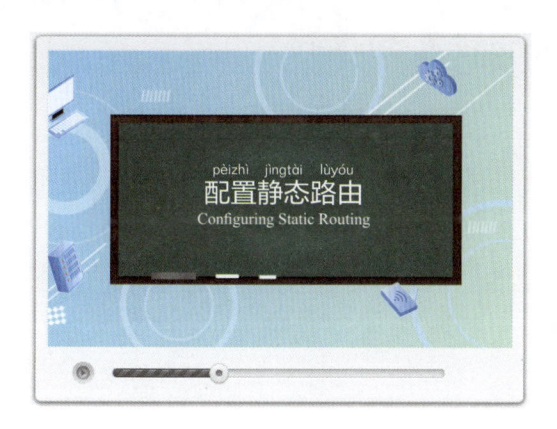

配置静态路由 Configuring Static Routing

实训目的 Training purpose

掌握静态路由配置步骤，并能独立完成配置，让计算机之间可以相互通信。

To master the steps of static routing configuration, and be able to complete the configuration independently to enable computers to communicate with each other.

实训组织 Training organization

每组 4 人，选出一个组长。

Students work in groups of 4. Each group chooses a group leader.

实训内容 Training content

配置静态路由。

Configuring static routing.

实训步骤 Training steps

① 将参加人员分成若干小组，每组 4 人。

　Divide the students into groups of 4.

② 第一个人安装 eNSP 软件。

　The first student installs the eNSP software.

③ 第二个人绘制拓扑图，准备配置静态路由。

　The second student draws the topology diagram and prepares for configuring the static routing.

④ 第三个人启动设备，并配置静态路由。

　The third student starts the device and configures the static routing.

⑤ 第四个人测试计算机连通性。

　The fourth student tests the connectivity of computers.

⑥ 实训结束，总结评价。

　The teacher makes a summary and an evaluation, and ends the training.

第五部分 Part 5 单元小结 Unit Summary

词语 cíyǔ Vocabulary

普通词语 General Vocabulary

先	xiān	conj.	first

专业词语 Specialized Vocabulary

1.	静态路由	jìngtài lùyóu	phr.	static routing
	静态	jìngtài	adj.	static
	路由	lùyóu	n.	routing
2.	手工配置	shǒugōng pèizhì	phr.	manual configuration
	手工	shǒugōng	n.	handwork
3.	路由信息	lùyóu xìnxī	phr.	routing information
4.	eNSP			Enterprise Network Simulation Platform (a network emulator from Huawei)
5.	网关	wǎngguān	n.	gateway

补充专业词语 Supplementary Specialized Vocabulary

1.	相互通信	xiānghù tōngxìn	phr.	communicate with each other
	相互	xiānghù	adv.	mutually
2.	私有 IP 地址	sīyǒu IP dìzhǐ	phr.	private IP address
	私有	sīyǒu	v.	own privately
3.	NAT			Network Address Translation

句子 jùzi Sentences

静态路由配置流程：

第一步，下载并安装 eNSP 软件。

第二步，打开 eNSP 软件，绘制网络拓扑图。

第三步，启动所需设备。

第四步，打开路由器模拟器，进行静态路由配置。

第五步，打开计算机模拟器，设置 IP 地址、子网掩码和网关。

第六步，保存配置，并测试计算机连通性。

10 IP 地址管理
IP Address Management

开启接口地址池的 DHCP 服务器功能的操作步骤
Operation Steps of Activating the DHCP Server Function of the Interface Address Pool

```
The device is running!
############
<Huawei>system-view
Enter system view, return user view with Ctrl+Z
```

执行命令 systm-view，进入系统视图
execute the system-view command to enter the system view

```
[Huawei]interface gigabitethernet 0/0/1
```

执行命令 interface interface-type interface-number，进入接口视图
execute the interface interface-type interface-number command to enter the interface view

```
[Huawei-GigabitEthernet0/0/1]ip address 10.0.10.1 255.255.255.224
```

执行命令 ip address ip-address{mask|mask-length}，配置接口的 IP 地址
execute the ip address ip-address{mask|mask-length} command to configure the IP address of the interface

```
[Huawei-GigabitEthernet0/0/1]dhcp select interface
```

执行命令 dhcp select interface，开启接口地址池的 DHCP 服务器功能
execute the dhcp select interface command to activate the DHCP server function of the interface address pool

121

> **题解　Introduction**
>
> 1. 学习内容：DHCP 技术的基本概念、配置方法和作用。
>   Learning content: The basic concept, configuration method and functions of DHCP technology.
> 2. 知识目标：掌握 DHCP 技术相关的核心词汇，学习汉字的笔画（总表）、笔顺规则（总表）和汉字结构（总表），学写相关汉字。
>   Knowledge objectives: To master the core vocabulary related to DHCP technology, learn about the general table of strokes, principles of stroke order and structures of Chinese characters, and write the related characters.
> 3. 技能目标：学会 DHCP 的配置。
>   Skill objective: To learn the configuration of DHCP.

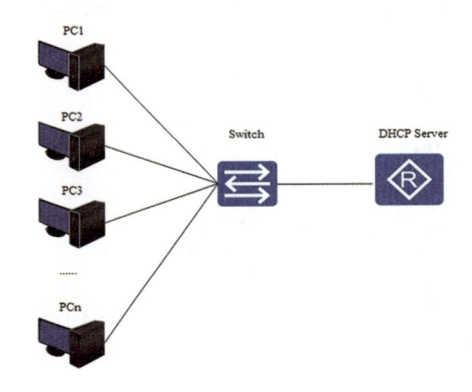

第一部分　Part 1

课文　Texts

一、热身　rèshēn　Warm-up

1. 下列所给的是 DHCP 相关图示，请给词语选择对应的图示。
   The following are the icons related to DHCP. Please match the words and phrases with corresponding icons.

   A.

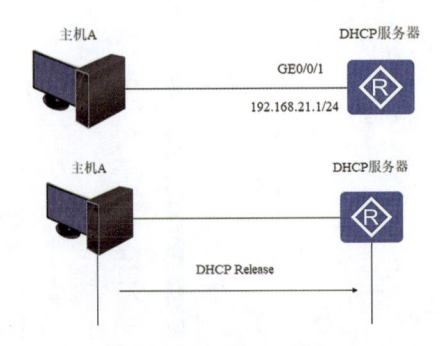

   B.

IP 地址管理
IP Address Management

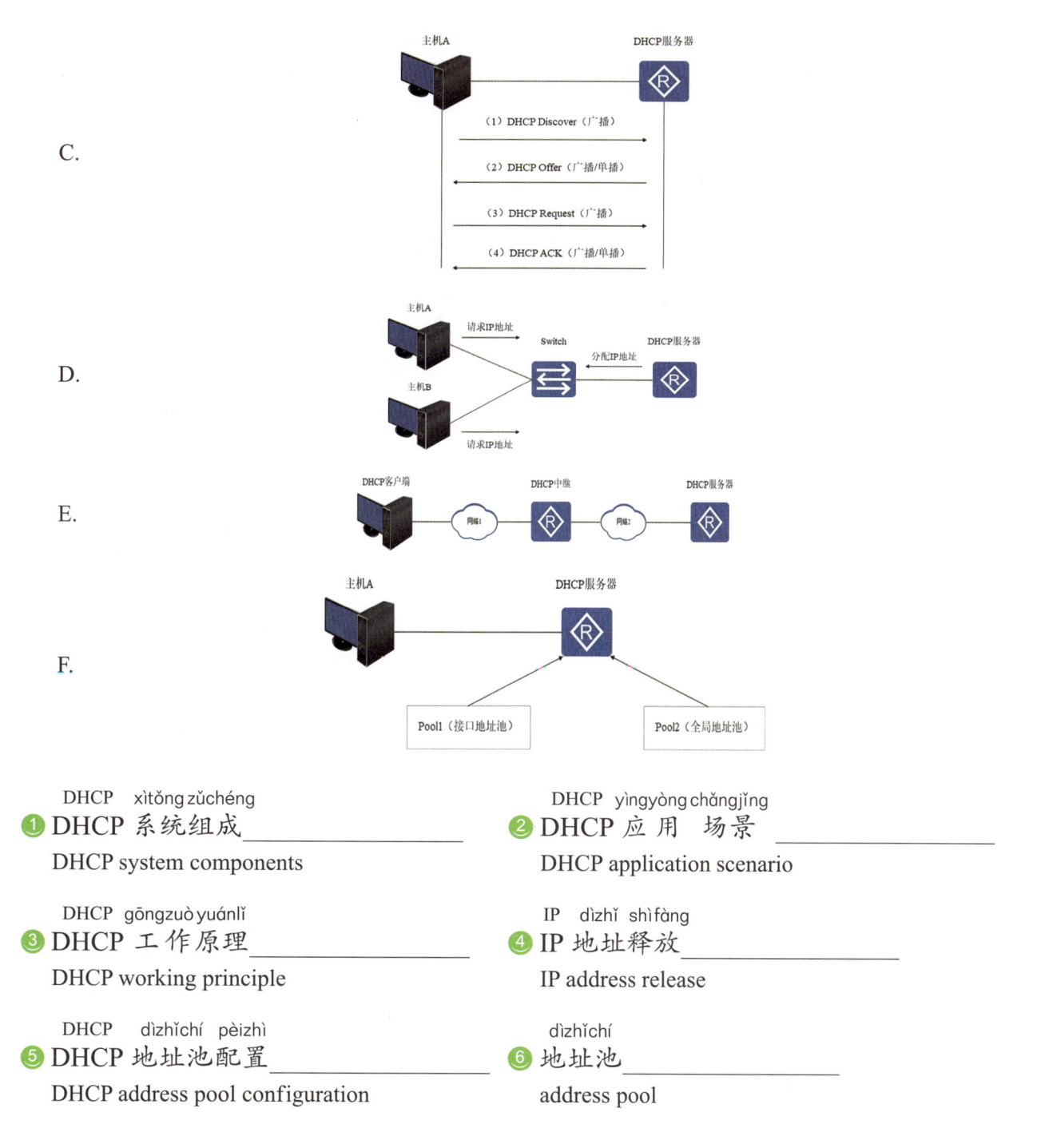

C.

D.

E.

F.

① DHCP 系统组成_____
    DHCP xìtǒng zǔchéng
    DHCP system components

② DHCP 应用 场景_____
    DHCP yìngyòng chǎngjǐng
    DHCP application scenario

③ DHCP 工作原理_____
    DHCP gōngzuò yuánlǐ
    DHCP working principle

④ IP 地址释放_____
    IP dìzhǐ shìfàng
    IP address release

⑤ DHCP 地址池配置_____
    DHCP dìzhǐchí pèizhì
    DHCP address pool configuration

⑥ 地址池_____
    dìzhǐchí
    address pool

2. 观看介绍 DHCP 的基本工作流程的视频，将下列这些命令与其对应含义连线。
Watch the video introducing the basic working process of DHCP, and connect the following commands to the corresponding meanings.

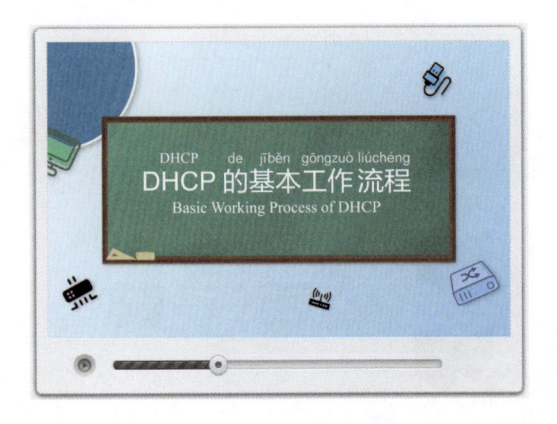

❶ fāxiàn jiēduàn
发现阶段
discovery phase

❷ tígōng jiēduàn
提供阶段
provision phase

❸ qǐngqiú jiēduàn
请求阶段
request phase

❹ quèrèn jiēduàn
确认阶段
confirmation phase

A. DHCP Request（xiāoxi 消息）
DHCP Request Information

B. DHCP Discover（xiāoxi 消息）
DHCP Discover Information

C. DHCP Ack（xiāoxi 消息）
DHCP Ack Information

D. DHCP Offer（xiāoxi 消息）
DHCP Offer Information

二、课文 kèwén Texts

A 🎧 10-01

徒弟：师傅，DHCP 是什么？

师傅：DHCP 是一种用于集中对用户 IP 地址进行动态管理和配置的技术。

徒弟：DHCP 技术有什么功能？

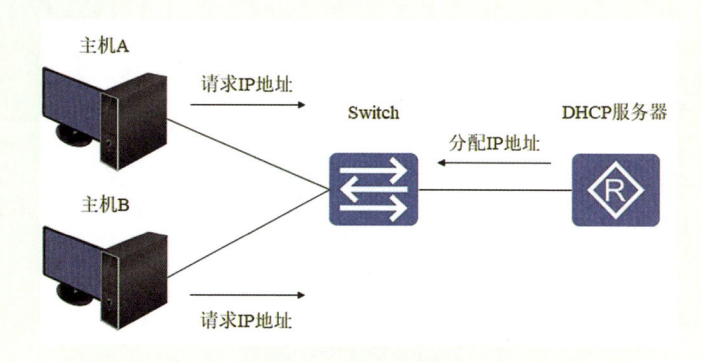

师傅：它可以降低客户端的配置和维护成本，并能够实现集中管理功能。

中文＋计算机网络技术（中级）

译文 yìwén Text in English

Apprentice: Master, what is DHCP?
Master: DHCP is a technology used to centrally manage and configure user IP addresses dynamically.
Apprentice: What are the functions of DHCP technology?
Master: It can reduce the configuration and maintenance cost of the clients, and realize the centralized management function.

普通词语 pǔtōng cíyǔ General Vocabulary 🎧 10-02

1.	用于	yòngyú	phr.	be used for
2.	集中	jízhōng	adj.	centralized, concentrated
3.	对	duì	prep.	to, for
4.	降低	jiàngdī	v.	reduce
5.	维护	wéihù	v.	maintain
6.	成本	chéngběn	n.	cost
7.	能够	nénggòu	v.	be able to

专业词语 zhuānyè cíyǔ Specialized Vocabulary 🎧 10-03

1.	动态管理	dòngtài guǎnlǐ	phr.	dynamic management
	动态	dòngtài	adj.	dynamic
	管理	guǎnlǐ	v.	manage
2.	DHCP 技术	DHCP jìshù	phr.	DHCP technology
3.	客户端	kèhùduān	phr.	client side

B 🎧 10-04

课文 B
kèwén B
Text B

túdì: Shīfu, DHCP kèhùduān de zuòyòng shì shénme?
徒弟：师傅，DHCP 客户端的 作用 是什么？

IP 地址管理 10
IP Address Management

师傅：DHCP 客户端的作用是通过 DHCP 协议请求获取 IP 地址等网络参数。

徒弟：DHCP 服务器的作用是什么？

师傅：DHCP 服务器是负责为 DHCP 客户端分配网络参数的设备，处理来自 DHCP 客户端的多种不同请求。

徒弟：那地址池的作用是什么？

师傅：地址池中的地址可以动态地分配给网络中的客户机使用。

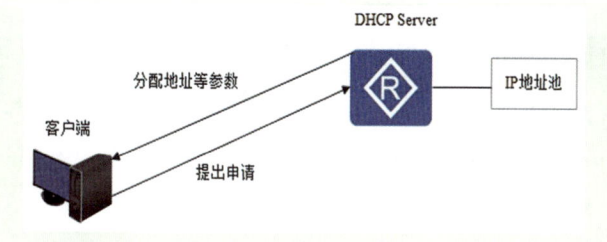

译文 yìwén Text in English

Apprentice: Master, what is the function of the DHCP client?

Master: The function of the DHCP client is to request to obtain IP address and other network parameters through DHCP protocol.

Apprentice: What is the function of the the DHCP server?

Master: The DHCP server is a device responsible for assigning network parameters to DHCP clients and processing a variety of requests from DHCP clients.

Apprentice: What is the function of the address pool?

Master: The addresses in the address pool can be dynamically assigned to the clients in the network.

普通词语 pǔtōng cíyǔ General Vocabulary 🎧 10-05

1.	请求	qǐngqiú	v.	request
2.	获取	huòqǔ	v.	obtain
3.	负责	fùzé	v.	be responsible for
4.	为	wèi	prep.	for
5.	分配	fēnpèi	v.	assign, allocate
6.	处理	chǔlǐ	v.	handle

127

7.	来自	láizì	v.	be from
8.	地	de	part.	a particle word used after a word or phrase to indicate adverbial function
9.	给	gěi	prep.	to, for

专业词语 zhuānyè cíyǔ Specialized Vocabulary 🎧 10-06

1.	DHCP 客户端	DHCP kèhùduān	phr.	DHCP client side
2.	DHCP 协议	DHCP xiéyì	phr.	DHCP protocol
3.	网络参数	wǎngluò cānshù	phr.	network parameter
4.	DHCP 服务器	DHCP fúwùqì	phr.	DHCP server
5.	地址池	dìzhǐchí	phr.	address pool
	池	chí	n.	pool
6.	客户机	kèhùjī	phr.	client
	客户	kèhù	n.	client

三、视听说 shì-tīng-shuō Viewing, Listening and Speaking

1. 观看介绍地址池创建方式及其区别的视频，并根据视频内容选择正确的答案。
Watch the video introducing the creation method of address pools and their differences, and choose the correct answers according to the content of the video.

　　　　suǒyǒu jiēkǒu　　　　quánjú　　　　　wǎngduàn　　　　jiēkǒu
A. 所有接口　　B. 全局　　　C. 网段　　　D. 接口
　all interfaces　　global　　network segment　　interface

❶ ___ 地址池 (dìzhǐchí) address pool	IP 地址与此接口的 IP 地址属于同一 ❸ _____。 IP dìzhǐ yǔ cǐ jiēkǒu de IP dìzhǐ shǔyú tóngyī The IP address falls under the same _____ as the IP address of this interface.
	地址只能分配给此接口下的客户端。 Dìzhǐ zhǐ néng fēnpèi gěi cǐ jiēkǒu xià de kèhùduān. The addresses can only be assigned to clients under this interface.

128

| ❷ _____ 地址池 address pool | dìzhǐ kěyǐ fēnpèi gěi shèbèi   xià de kèhùduān.
地址可以分配给设备 ❹ _____ 下的客户端。
The addresses can be assigned to clients under _____ of the device. |

2. 说一说 Let's talk.

说一说地址池创建的两种方式及它们的区别。

Talk about the two methods to create address pools and their differences.

四、学以致用 xuéyǐzhìyòng Practicing What You Have Learnt

观看介绍开启接口地址池的 DHCP 服务器功能的视频，选择正确的步骤内容。

Watch the video introducing the operation of activating the DHCP server function of the interface address pool, and choose the correct steps.

A. IP 地址 (IP dìzhǐ) — IP address
B. 接口视图 (jiēkǒu shìtú) — interface view
C. 接口地址池 (jiēkǒu dìzhǐchí) — interface address pool
D. 系统视图 (xìtǒng shìtú) — system view

❶ 执行命令 system-view，进入 _____
Execute the system-view command to enter _____

❷ 执行命令 interface interface-type interface-number，进入 _____
Execute the interface interface-type interface-number command to enter _____

❸ 执行命令 ip ip-address{mask | mask-length}，配置接口的 _____
Execute the ip ip-address{mask | mask-length} command to configure the _____ of the interface

❹ 执行命令 dhcp select interface，开启 _____ 的 DHCP 服务器功能
Execute the dhcp select interface command to activate the DHCP server function of the _____.

五、小知识 xiǎo zhīshi Tips

DHCP 分配 IP 地址的三种方式

DHCP 有三种分配 IP 地址的方式：（1）自动分配方式，DHCP 服务器为主机指定一个永久性的 IP 地址，一旦 DHCP 客户端第一次成功地从 DHCP 服务器端租用到 IP 地址后，就可以永久性地使用该地址。（2）动态分配方式，DHCP 服务器给主机指定一个具有时间限制的 IP 地址，时间到期或主机明确表示放弃该地址时，该地址可以被其他主机使用。（3）手工分配方式，客户端的 IP 地址是由网络管理员指定的，DHCP 服务器只是将指定的 IP 地址告诉客户端主机。三种地址分配方式中，只有动态分配可以重复使用客户端不再需要的地址。

Three Methods of Assigning IP Addresses by DHCP

DHCP has three methods of assigning IP addresses: (1) Automatic assignment. The DHCP server assigns a permanent IP address to the host. Once the DHCP client side successfully rents an IP address from the DHCP server side for the first time, it can use the IP address permanently. (2) Dynamic assignment. The DHCP server assigns a time-limited IP address to the host. When the assignment is due or the host explicitly gives up this IP address, this address can be used by another host. (3) Manual assignment. The IP address of the client side is assigned by the network administrator, and the DHCP server only informs the client host the specified IP address. In these three IP address assignment methods, only dynamic assignment allows the IP addresses that are no longer needed by the client side to be reused.

补充专业词语 bǔchōng zhuānyè cíyǔ Supplementary Specialized Vocabulary   🎧 10-07

1.	工作原理	gōngzuò yuánlǐ	phr.	working principle
2.	地址释放	dìzhǐ shìfàng	phr.	address release
3.	动态分配	dòngtài fēnpèi	phr.	dynamic assignment

第二部分　Part 2
汉字　Chinese Characters

一、汉字知识　Hànzì zhīshi　Knowledge about Chinese Characters

1. 汉字的笔画（总表） Strokes of Chinese characters (general table)

一	丨	丿	丶	、	㇆	㇄
㇗	㇀	㇉	㇌	㇊	㇎	㇋
㇁	㇏	㇂	㇈	ㄱ	乙	㇅
㇆	㇇	㇐	㇑	㇒	㇓	㇔

2. 汉字的笔顺（总表） Stroke orders of Chinese characters (general table)

笔顺规则 Rules of stroke orders	例字 Examples
先横后竖	十
先撇后捺	人、八
先上后下	三
先左后右	人
先中间后两边	小
先外边后里边	月、问
先外后里再封口	国、日

3. 汉字的结构（总表） Structures of Chinese characters (general table)

结构类型 Structure types	结构图示 Illustrations	例字 Examples
独体结构	□	生、不
品字形结构	▤	品
上下结构	▤ ▤	爸、节
上中下结构	▤	意
左右结构	▥	银、饭
左中右结构	▥	班、微
全包围结构	□	国
半包围结构	▢ ▢ ▢ ▢	医、边、问、唐、凶

二、汉字认读与书写　Hànzì rèndú yǔ shūxiě　The Recognition and Writing of Chinese Characters

认读下列汉字构成的词语，并试着写汉字。
Read the words composed of the following Chinese characters, and try to write them.

动态管理　　网络参数　　地址池　　服务器

动				态				管				理			
网				络				参				数			
地				址				池				服			
务				器											

第三部分　Part 3　日常用语 Daily Expressions

1. 谢谢你的礼物，我很喜欢。Xièxie nǐ de lǐwù, wǒ hěn xǐhuan. Thanks for your gift. I like it very much.
2. 谢谢您的邀请，我一定去。Xièxie nín de yāoqǐng, wǒ yídìng qù. Thanks for your invitation. I will go for sure.
3. 我该走了，再见。Wǒ gāi zǒu le, zàijiàn. I've got to go. Bye.

第四部分　Part 4　单元实训 Unit Practical Training

DHCP 的配置
Configuration of DHCP

DHCP 的配置 Configuration of DHCP

实训目的 Training purpose

学会 DHCP 的配置。

To learn the configuration of DHCP.

实训组织 Training organization

每组 3 ~ 5 人，选出一个组长。

Students work in groups of 3-5. Each group chooses a group leader.

实训内容 Training content

DHCP 的配置。

Configuration of DHCP.

实训步骤 Training steps

❶ 如下图所示，在 eNSP 软件中绘制网络拓扑图。

As shown in the graph below, draw the network topology in the eNSP software.

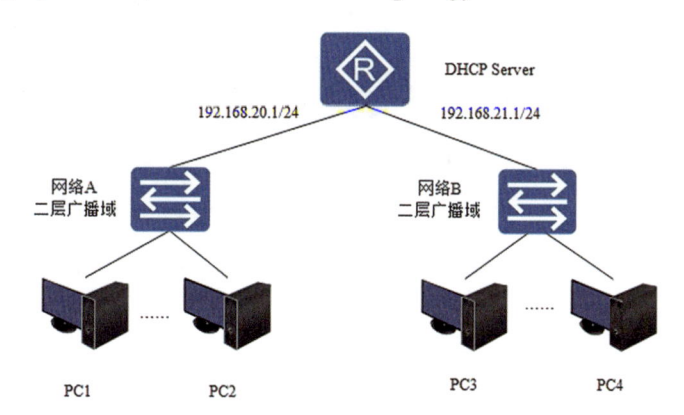

❷ 路由器配置 DHCP 服务。

The router configures DHCP service.

❸ 设置 PC1、PC2、PC3、PC4 的网络地址。

Set the network addresses of PC1, PC2, PC3 and PC4.

❹ PC1、PC2、PC3、PC4 连通性测试。

Connectivity test of PC1, PC2, PC3 and PC4.

❺ DHCP 进阶练习，如下图所示。

DHCP advanced practice, as shown in the graph below.

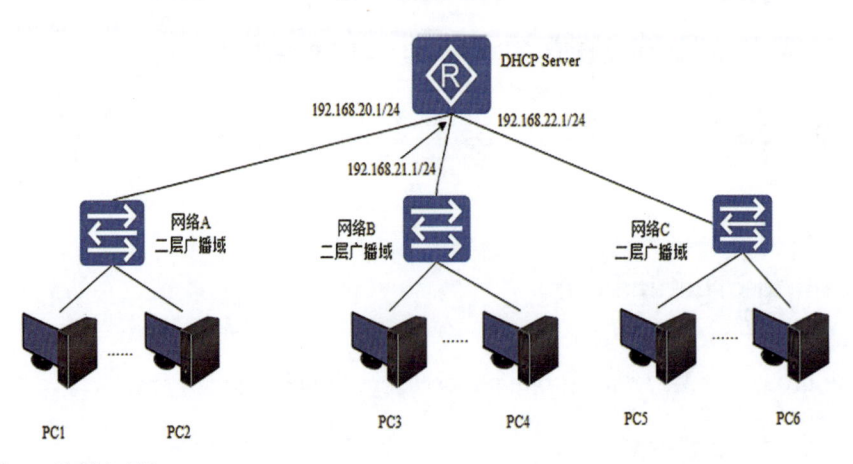

❻ 实训结束，总结评价。
The teacher makes a summary and an evaluation, and ends the training.

第五部分　Part 5　单元小结　Unit Summary

词语 cíyǔ Vocabulary

普通词语　General Vocabulary

1.	用于	yòngyú	phr.	be used for
2.	集中	jízhōng	adj.	centralized, concentrated
3.	对	duì	prep.	to, for
4.	降低	jiàngdī	v.	reduce
5.	维护	wéihù	v.	maintain
6.	成本	chéngběn	n.	cost
7.	能够	nénggòu	v.	be able to
8.	请求	qǐngqiú	v.	request
9.	获取	huòqǔ	v.	obtain
10.	负责	fùzé	v.	be responsible for
11.	为	wèi	prep.	for
12.	分配	fēnpèi	v.	assign, allocate
13.	处理	chǔlǐ	v.	handle
14.	来自	láizì	v.	be from
15.	地	de	part.	a particle word used after a word or phrase to indicate adverbial function
16.	给	gěi	prep.	to, for

专业词语　Specialized Vocabulary

1.	动态管理	dòngtài guǎnlǐ	phr.	dynamic management
	动态	dòngtài	adj.	dynamic
	管理	guǎnlǐ	v.	manage
2.	DHCP 技术	DHCP jìshù	phr.	DHCP technology
3.	客户端	kèhùduān	phr.	client side
4.	DHCP 客户端	DHCP kèhùduān	phr.	DHCP client
5.	DHCP 协议	DHCP xiéyì	phr.	DHCP protocol
6.	网络参数	wǎngluò cānshù	phr.	network parameter
7.	DHCP 服务器	DHCP fúwùqì	phr.	DHCP server
8.	地址池	dìzhǐchí	phr.	address pool
	池	chí	n.	pool
9.	客户机	kèhùjī	phr.	client
	客户	kèhù	n.	client

补充专业词语　Supplementary Specialized Vocabulary

1.	工作原理	gōngzuò yuánlǐ	phr.	working principle
2	地址释放	dìzhǐ shìfàng	phr.	address release
3	动态分配	dòngtài fēnpèi	phr.	dynamic assignment

句子 jùzi Sentences

1. DHCP 是一种用于集中对用户 IP 地址进行动态管理和配置的技术。
2. DHCP 技术可以降低客户端的配置和维护成本，并能够实现集中管理功能。
3. DHCP 客户端的作用是通过 DHCP 协议请求获取 IP 地址等网络参数。
4. DHCP 服务器是负责为 DHCP 客户端分配网络参数的设备，处理来自 DHCP 客户端的多种不同请求。
5. 地址池中的地址可以动态地分配给网络中的客户机使用。

附录　Appendix

词语总表 Vocabulary

序号	单词	拼音	词性	词义	普通G/专业S	在第几课
1	按	àn	v.	press	G	3A
2	版本特性	bǎnběn tèxìng	phr.	version property	S	1
3	本身	běnshēn	pron.	oneself	G	8A
4	比如	bǐrú	v.	take sth. for example	G	4A
5	比特	bǐtè	n.	bit	S	8B
6	必备	bìbèi	v.	be necessary	G	2B
7	编号	biānhào	n.	number	S	4
8	标签栏	biāoqiānlán	phr.	tab bar	S	2
9	标识	biāoshí	v.	identify, indicate	G	8A
10	表示	biǎoshì	v.	indicate, show	G	8B
11	不同	bù tóng	phr.	different	G	4A
12	部署	bùshǔ	v.	deploy	G	1B
13	才	cái	adv.	used to indicate that sth. happens only on certain conditions	G	5B
14	采用	cǎiyòng	v.	adopt	G	3B
15	侧	cè	n.	side	G	2B
16	插	chā	v.	plug	G	2B
17	插槽	chācáo	n.	slot	S	6
18	产品	chǎnpǐn	n.	product	G	1A
19	长度	chángdù	n.	length	G	8B
20	称为	chēngwéi	phr.	be named	G	3A
21	成本	chéngběn	n.	cost	G	10A
22	池	chí	n.	pool	S	10B
23	重	chóng	adv.	again	S	5A
24	重命名	chóng mìng//míng	phr.	rename	S	5A
25	重启	chóngqǐ	phr.	restart	S	6A
26	重新	chóngxīn	adv.	again	G	6B
27	出厂	chū//chǎng	v.	(of products) be dispatched from the factory	G	3B
28	初始	chūshǐ	n.	inception, initial stage	G	2A
29	处理	chǔlǐ	v.	handle	G	10B
30	串口线	chuànkǒuxiàn	phr.	serial line	S	2

（续表）

序号	单词	拼音	词性	词义	普通G/专业S	在第几课
31	从而	cóng'ér	conj.	thus, thereby	G	7A
32	存储器	cúnchǔqì	n.	memory	S	5
33	当前	dāngqián	n.	current time, present	G	3B
34	地	de	part.	a particle word used after a word or phrase to indicate adverbial function	G	10B
35	地方	dìfang	n.	place	G	6B
36	地址	dìzhǐ	n.	address	S	7B
37	地址池	dìzhǐchí	phr.	address pool	S	10B
38	地址释放	dìzhǐ shìfàng	phr.	address release	S	10
39	点分十进制	diǎnfēn shíjìnzhì	phr.	dotted decimal notation	S	8B
40	动态	dòngtài	adj.	dynamic	S	10A
41	动态分配	dòngtài fēnpèi	phr.	dynamic assignment	S	10
42	动态管理	dòngtài guǎnlǐ	phr.	dynamic management	S	10A
43	都	dōu	adv.	all, both	G	2B
44	端口	duānkǒu	n.	port	S	7B
45	对	duì	adj.	right	G	8B
46	对	duì	prep.	to, for	G	10A
47	二进制	èrjìnzhì	phr.	binary system	S	8B
48	返回	fǎnhuí	v.	return	G	3A
49	方括号	fāngkuòhào	phr.	square bracket	G	3A
50	方式	fāngshì	n.	mode	S	4A
51	分配	fēnpèi	v.	assign, allocate	G	10B
52	分为	fēnwéi	phr.	be divided into	G	1B
53	负责	fùzé	v.	be responsible for	G	10B
54	复制	fùzhì	v.	copy	S	5A
55	高	gāo	adj.	high	S	1A
56	个	gè	m.	a measure word	G	1B
57	个数	gèshù	phr.	number	G	8B
58	给	gěi	prep.	to, for	G	10B
59	根	gēn	m.	a measure word for something long and thin	G	2B
60	根据	gēnjù	prep.	according to	G	7B
61	根目录	gēnmùlù	phr.	root directory	S	6B
62	工作原理	gōngzuò yuánlǐ	phr.	working principle	S	10

(续表)

序号	单词	拼音	词性	词义	普通G/专业S	在第几课
63	工作组	gōngzuòzǔ	n.	working group	S	7A
64	功能	gōngnéng	n.	function	G	1B
65	关键	guānjiàn	n.	key	S	1B
66	关键字	guānjiànzì	phr.	keyword	S	1B
67	管理	guǎnlǐ	v.	manage	S	10A
68	广	guǎng	adj.	wide	G	7B
69	广播流	guǎngbōliú	phr.	broadcast stream	S	7
70	广泛	guǎngfàn	adj.	wide	G	7B
71	过程	guòchéng	n.	process	G	4A
72	后接	hòu jiē	phr.	be followed by	G	7A
73	华为公司	Huáwéi Gōngsī	pn.	Huawei Company	G	8B
74	划分	huàfēn	v.	divide	G	1A
75	或	huò	conj.	or	G	3A
76	或者	huòzhě	conj.	or	G	8B
77	获取	huòqǔ	v.	obtain	G	10B
78	基于	jīyú	prep.	on account of	S	7B
79	级别	jíbié	n.	level	G	1B
80	即	jí	adv.	i.e., namely	G	8A
81	集中	jízhōng	adj.	centralized, concentrated	G	10A
82	计算	jìsuàn	v.	calculate	G	8B
83	记住	jìzhù	phr.	remember	G	5B
84	技术	jìshù	n.	technology	S	7A
85	尖括号	jiānkuòhào	phr.	angle bracket	G	3A
86	简称	jiǎnchēng	n.	abbreviation	G	7A
87	键	jiàn	n.	key	G	3A
88	将	jiāng	prep.	used to introduce the object before the verb	G	6A
89	降低	jiàngdī	v.	reduce	G	10A
90	交换机	jiāohuànjī	n.	switch	S	5B
91	叫	jiào	v.	be called	G	7A
92	接	jiē	v.	follow	G	8B
93	接口	jiēkǒu	n.	be interface	G	2B
94	接口视图	jiēkǒu shìtú	phr.	interface view	S	1

（续表）

序号	单词	拼音	词性	词义	普通G/专业S	在第几课
95	仅	jǐn	adv.	only	G	3B
96	进入	jìnrù	v.	enter	G	3A
97	进行	jìnxíng	v.	proceed	G	3B
98	静态	jìngtài	adj.	static	S	9A
99	静态路由	jìngtài lùyóu	phr.	static routing	S	9A
100	具体	jùtǐ	adj.	specific	G	7B
101	绝对编号	juéduì biānhào	phr.	absolute number	S	4
102	可靠性	kěkàoxìng	n.	reliability	S	1A
103	可扩展性	kěkuòzhǎnxìng	n.	extensibility	S	1A
104	客户	kèhù	n.	client	S	10B
105	客户端	kèhùduān	phr.	client side	S	10A
106	客户机	kèhùjī	phr.	client	S	10B
107	控制	kòngzhì	v.	control	G	4A
108	口	kǒu	n.	port	S	2A
109	扩展	kuòzhǎn	v.	extend	S	6A
110	扩展名	kuòzhǎnmíng	phr.	extension	S	6A
111	括号	kuòhào	n.	bracket	G	3A
112	来自	láizì	v.	be from	G	10B
113	了解	liǎojiě	v.	understand	G	3B
114	类	lèi	m.	type, kind	G	7B
115	例	lì	n.	example	G	5B
116	例如	lìrú	v.	quote an example	G	3A
117	连续	liánxù	v.	go on uninterruptedly	G	8B
118	另	lìng	pron.	other	G	2B
119	流量	liúliàng	n.	traffic, flow	S	7
120	路由	lùyóu	n.	routing	S	9A
121	路由信息	lùyóu xìnxī	phr.	routing information	S	9A
122	逻辑	luóji	n.	logic	S	7A
123	没	méi	v.	not have	G	6B
124	没有	méiyǒu	v.	not have	G	2A
125	每	měi	pron.	each	G	4A
126	每个	měi gè	phr.	every	G	4A
127	名	míng	n.	name	S	6A

(续表)

序号	单词	拼音	词性	词义	普通G/专业S	在第几课
128	名称	míngchēng	n.	name	G	3A
129	命令行	mìnglìngháng	phr.	command line	S	1B
130	命名	mìng//míng	v.	name	S	5A
131	目录	mùlù	n.	directory	S	5A
132	那么	nàme	conj.	then	G	7B
133	内	nèi	n.	inside	G	7A
134	内存	nèicún	n.	RAM	G	6A
135	内容	nèiróng	n.	content	G	3A
136	能够	nénggòu	v.	be able to	G	10A
137	配置信息	pèizhì xìnxī	phr.	configuration information	S	6A
138	配置指令	pèizhì zhǐlìng	phr.	configuration instruction	S	3
139	其他	qítā	pron.	other	G	5B
140	启动	qǐdòng	v.	start	S	5B
141	切换	qiēhuàn	v.	switch	G	3A
142	情况	qíngkuàng	n.	situation, condition	G	3A
143	请求	qǐngqiú	v.	request	G	10B
144	权限	quánxiàn	n.	permission	S	4
145	缺省	quēshěng	v.	default	G	3A
146	让	ràng	v.	let, make	G	6B
147	人	rén	n.	people	G	6B
148	认证	rènzhèng	v.	authenticate, certify	S	4A
149	认证方式	rènzhèng fāngshì	phr.	authentication mode	S	4A
150	日期	rìqī	n.	date	G	3B
151	若干	ruògān	pron.	a number of, several	G	8B
152	删除	shānchú	v.	delete	S	5A
153	上	shang	n.	upside	G	2B
154	设备端	shèbèiduān	phr.	on-device, device side	S	2A
155	时	shí	n.	(the duration of) time	G	3B
156	时间	shíjiān	n.	time	G	3B
157	时区	shíqū	n.	time zone	S	3B
158	时钟	shízhōng	n.	clock	G	3B
159	实际	shíjì	adj.	practical	G	7B
160	实现	shíxiàn	v.	realize	G	2A

（续表）

序号	单词	拼音	词性	词义	普通G/专业S	在第几课
161	世界	shìjiè	n.	world	G	3B
162	世界时	shìjièshí	n.	universal time	S	3B
163	视图	shìtú	n.	view	S	1
164	手动	shǒudòng	adj.	manual	S	6B
165	手工	shǒugōng	n.	handwork	S	9A
166	手工配置	shǒugōng pèizhì	phr.	manual configuration	S	9A
167	属于	shǔyú	v.	belong to	G	4A
168	数	shù	n.	number	G	8B
169	数据	shùjù	n.	data	S	1A
170	私有	sīyǒu	v.	own privately	S	9
171	私有IP地址	sīyǒu IP dìzhǐ	phr.	private IP address	S	9
172	随时	suíshí	adv.	at any time	G	6B
173	所	suǒ	part.	used before the verb to indicate the receiver of the action	G	3B
174	所有	suǒyǒu	adj.	all	G	2B
175	它们	tāmen	pron.	they	G	3A
176	通常	tōngcháng	adv.	usually	G	8B
177	通过	tōngguò	prep.	through	G	2A
178	通信	tōngxìn	n.	communication	S	1A
179	通用	tōngyòng	adj.	all-purpose, universal	G	1A
180	统一	tǒngyī	adj.	universal, unified	G	3B
181	外部	wàibù	n.	outside	S	5
182	外部存储器	wàibù cúnchǔqì	phr.	external memory	S	5
183	完成	wán//chéng	v.	complete	G	1B
184	晚上	wǎnshang	n.	night	G	6B
185	网段	wǎngduàn	n.	network segment	S	7A
186	网关	wǎngguān	n.	gateway	S	9B
187	网络	wǎngluò	n.	network	G	1A
188	网络参数	wǎngluò cānshù	phr.	network parameter	S	10B
189	网络号	wǎngluòhào	phr.	net ID	S	8A
190	维护	wéihù	v.	maintain	G	10A
191	为	wèi	prep.	for	G	10B
192	为什么	wèi shénme	phr.	why	G	2A

（续表）

序号	单词	拼音	词性	词义	普通G/专业S	在第几课
193	文件	wénjiàn	n.	file	S	5A
194	希望	xīwàng	v.	hope	G	6B
195	系列	xìliè	n.	series	G	4A
196	系统	xìtǒng	n.	system	S	1A
197	系统时钟	xìtǒng shízhōng	phr.	system clock	S	3B
198	系统视图	xìtǒng shìtú	phr.	system view	S	1
199	下	xià	n.	being in	G	2A
200	先	xiān	conj.	first	G	9B
201	显示	xiǎnshì	v.	display	S	5A
202	相对编号	xiāngduì biānhào	phr.	relative number	S	4
203	相互	xiānghù	adv.	mutually	S	9
204	相互通信	xiānghù tōngxìn	phr.	communicate with each other	S	9
205	相"与"运算	xiāng "yǔ" yùnsuàn	phr.	"AND" operation	S	8
206	小时制	xiǎoshízhì	phr.	hour system	G	3B
207	协调	xiétiáo	v./adj.	coordinate; coordinated	S	3B
208	协调世界时	xiétiáo shìjièshí	phr.	coordinated universal time	S	3B
209	协议	xiéyì	n.	protocol	S	7B
210	行为	xíngwéi	n.	behavior	G	4A
211	形式	xíngshì	n.	form	G	6A
212	性能	xìngnéng	n.	performance	S	1A
213	虚拟	xūnǐ	adj.	virtual	S	7A
214	业务	yèwù	n.	business	S	1B
215	移动	yídòng	v.	move	S	5A
216	以	yǐ	prep.	by, with	G	5B
217	一端	yì duān	phr.	one end	G	2B
218	因为	yīnwèi	conj.	because	G	2A
219	英文	Yīngwén	pn.	English	G	7A
220	应用	yìngyòng	v.	apply	G	7B
221	拥有	yōngyǒu	v.	own	G	4A
222	用	yòng	v.	use	G	2B
223	用户	yònghù	n.	user	S	1
224	用户级别	yònghù jíbié	phr.	user level	S	1
225	用户界面	yònghù jièmiàn	phr.	user interface	S	4A

（续表）

序号	单词	拼音	词性	词义	普通G/专业S	在第几课
226	用户视图	yònghù shìtú	phr.	user view	S	3A
227	用于	yòngyú	phr.	be used for	G	10A
228	优点	yōudiǎn	n.	advantage	G	1A
229	又	yòu	adv.	also	G	7A
230	右边	yòubian	n.	right	G	8A
231	与	yǔ	conj.	and	G	2A
232	原则	yuánzé	n.	principle	G	7B
233	运算	yùnsuàn	v.	operate, calculate	S	8
234	运用	yùnyòng	v.	use	G	7B
235	在	zài	v.	be in/on/at	G	3B
236	怎样	zěnyàng	pron.	how	G	1B
237	这样	zhèyàng	pron.	such	G	2A
238	支持	zhīchí	v.	support	G	3B
239	只	zhǐ	adv.	only	G	2A
240	指定	zhǐdìng	v.	specify	G	5A
241	中国	Zhōngguó	pn.	China	G	1A
242	中国时区	Zhōngguó shíqū	phr.	time zone of China	S	3
243	逐位	zhú wèi	phr.	bitwise	S	8
244	主机号	zhǔjīhào	phr.	host ID	S	8A
245	主机名	zhǔjīmíng	phr.	host name	S	3A
246	主要	zhǔyào	adj.	main	G	5A
247	状态	zhuàngtài	n.	state	G	2A
248	自己	zìjǐ	pron.	oneself	G	4A
249	字	zì	n.	word, character	S	1B
250	最	zuì	adv.	most	G	7B
251	最为	zuìwéi	adv.	most	G	7B
252	左边	zuǒbian	n.	left	G	8A
253	作用	zuòyòng	n.	function	G	1B
254	Console 口	Console kǒu	phr.	Console port	S	2A
255	DHCP 服务器	DHCP fúwùqì	phr.	DHCP server	S	10B
256	DHCP 技术	DHCP jìshù	phr.	DHCP technology	S	10A
257	DHCP 客户端	DHCP kèhùduān	phr.	DHCP client	S	10B
258	DHCP 协议	DHCP xiéyì	phr.	DHCP protocol	S	10B

143

（续表）

序号	单词	拼音	词性	词义	普通G/专业S	在第几课
259	eNSP			Enterprise Network Simulation Platform (a network emulator from Huawei)	S	9A
260	MAC			Media Access Control	S	7B
261	NAT			Network Address Translation	S	9
262	TCP/IP 网络	TCP/IP wǎngluò	phr.	TCP/IP network	S	8A
263	USB 口	USB kǒu	phr.	USB port	S	2B
264	VLAN			Virtual Local Area Network	S	7A
265	VRP			Versatile Routing Platform	S	1A
266	VTY 用户界面	VTY yònghù jièmiàn	phr.	VTY user interface	S	4B

视频脚本 Video Scripts

第一单元　命令行的使用

一、热身

小机器人：设备启动后，首先进入命令行界面；然后输入"system-view"命令，进入系统视图；输入"interface"命令，进入接口视图；再输入"quit"命令，从当前视图退出至上一层视图；最后输入"?"命令，获得在线帮助。

三、视听说

小机器人：VRP 命令级别分为 0～3 级。其中，0 级为参观级命令，用于测试网络是否连通等；1 级为监控级命令，用于查看网络状态和设备基本信息；2 级为配置级命令，用于业务配置；3 级为管理级命令，用于上传或者下载配置文件等。

四、学以致用

小机器人：VRP 命令级别在实际的运用中对应着不同的用户级别。VRP 用户权限分为 0～15 共 16 个级别。0 级可以操作网络诊断类命令和本设备访问其他设备的命令，1 级可以操作系统维护命令，2 级可以操作业务配置命令，3 级以上用户可以操作 VRP 系统的所有命令。

　　一般情况下，VRP 用户级别 0 对应 VRP 命令级 0，VRP 用户级别 1 对应 VRP 命令级 0、1，VRP 用户级别 2 对应 VRP 命令级 0、1、2，VRP 用户级别 3～15 对应 VRP 命令级 0、1、2、3。

第二单元　通过 Console 口登录设备

一、热身

徒弟：电脑与设备线如何连接？

师傅：设备线有两端，分别是 RJ45 接口和 USB 口。

徒弟：将 Console 线的 USB 口插入电脑的 USB 接口吗？

师傅：对的。然后，再将线缆 RJ45 接口插入设备 Console 端口。

三、视听说

徒弟：如何通过 Console 口登录设备并配置通信软件？

师傅：共有六个步骤。首先，鼠标右键点击"计算机"，选择"管理"；

　　　第二步，鼠标左键点击"设备管理器"，在右侧窗口选择"端口"；

　　　第三步，查看 COM 口编号；

　　　第四步，打开通信软件，点击"终端工具"标签栏，点击"新建连接"；

　　　第五步，设置"连接名称"，"类型"中选择对应的 COM 编号，点击"确定"；

　　　第六步，检查连接是否成功。

四、学以致用

徒弟：怎么通过 Console 口连接设备？

师傅：首先，用串口线连接电脑与设备；然后，打开电脑的"设备管理器"，并找到电脑上 USB 串行端口编号；接着，打开"IPOP"软件，点击"终端工具"标签，再设置连接参数，设备连接成功。

第三单元　设备的基本配置

一、热身

小机器人：这是用户视图，用户视图用来查看运行状态或其他参数；这是系统视图，系统视图用来配置设备的系统参数；这是接口视图，接口视图用来配置接口。

三、视听说

小机器人：如果现在设备所处的时区是北京所在的东八区，那么我们就这样设置时区和时间，然后显示当前时间，查看结果是否设置正确。比如，如果当前的日期为2021年6月10日，时间是凌晨1点04分00秒，则相应的配置指令应该是<NIIT_R1>clock datetime 01:04:00 2021-6-10。

四、学以致用

徒弟：IP地址非常重要，可是我们具体如何配置呢？

师傅：IP地址是针对设备接口的配置，通常一个接口配置一个IP地址。配置接口IP地址的命令中给出希望配置的IP地址。

徒弟：那具体的指令怎么写呢？

师傅：你看设置IP地址为10.1.1.100/24的设置指令为 ip address 10.1.1.100 255.255.255.0，其中IP地址为10.1.1.100，子网掩码为255.255.255.0。注意子网掩码要转换为点分十进制方式。

第四单元　用户界面配置

一、热身

徒弟：用户界面信息包括哪些？

师傅：包括相对编号、绝对编号、用户级别和认证方式等信息。

徒弟：如何在用户信息表中查看这些信息呢？

师傅：如图所示，"Idx"表示绝对编号，"Type"表示相对编号，"Privi"表示用户级别，"Auth"表示认证方式。

三、视听说

徒弟：如何配置VTY用户界面？

师傅：每个操作步骤都有具体的含义。首先，配置最大VTY用户界面数为15；

　　　第二步，进入VTY用户界面视图；

　　　第三步，配置认证方式为AAA；

　　　第四步，配置AAA用户名和密码；

　　　最后，配置用户可访问的业务类型。

四、学以致用

徒弟：配置用户界面时每个操作的含义是什么？

师傅：每个信息上面都有英文，比如，idle是不工作的状态，timeout是超时的意思。[Huawei-ui-vty0-14] idle-timeout 这个操作就是设置用户界面超时时长。再看下一个操作，[Huawei]user-interface maximum-vty，是什么意思呢？

徒弟：这个操作应该是设置最大VTY数目。

第五单元　文件系统管理

一、热身

小机器人：VRP文件系统主要用来创建、删除、修改、复制和显示文件及目录，文件和目录都存在于设备的外部存储器中。华为路由器支持的外部存储器一般为Flash卡和SD卡，交换机支持的外部存储器一般为Flash卡和CF卡。

三、视听说

徒弟：文件操作有哪些命令呢？

师傅：文件操作主要有复制文件、重命名文件、移动文件、删除文件等命令。

徒弟：如何复制一个文件呢？

师傅：启动交换机，用 copy 命令，比如把 patchfile.src 这个文件复制为 test.src 这个文件

    <Huawei>cd src

    <Huawei>dir

    <Huawei>copy patchfile.src test.src

徒弟：如何把 test.src 这个文件重新命名为其他文件名呢？

师傅：用 rename，比如把 test.src 重命名为 dest.src

    <Huawei>rename test.src dest.src

徒弟：如何把 dest.src 移动到其他目录呢？

师傅：创建一个子目录 sub，然后把 dest.src 移到 sub 目录

    <Huawei>mkdir sub

    <Huawei>move dest.src sub

徒弟：不想要 dest.src 文件了，如何删除呢？

师傅：用 delete 命令可以删除文件。

    <Huawei>cd sub

    <Huawei>delete dest.src

四、学以致用

徒弟：路由器如何对文件和目录进行操作？

师傅：第一步，运行 eNSP，启动路由器；

    第二步，用 dir 命令，查看当前目录下的信息；

    <Huawei>dir

    第三步，用 mkdir 命令，创建一个目录，目录名叫作 mydir；

    <Huawei>mkdir mydir

    第四步，用 cd 命令，修改用户当前的工作目录为 mydir。

    <Huawei>cd mydir

徒弟：进入 mydir 目录了，不想要 mydir 目录了，如何删除？

师傅：用 rmdir 命令，删除目录。如删除 mydir 目录。

    <Huawei>rmdir mydir

第六单元　配置文件管理

一、热身

小机器人：今天一起学习配置文件的知识。设备内存中配置的信息称为当前配置，设备断电或重启后，内存中原有的配置信息会消失。包含设备配置信息的文件称为配置文件，存储在设备的外部存储器中，文件名格式一般为"*.cfg"或"*.zip"。可以将当前配置保存到配置文件中，当设备重启时配置文件的内容可以被加载到内存，成为新的当前配置。

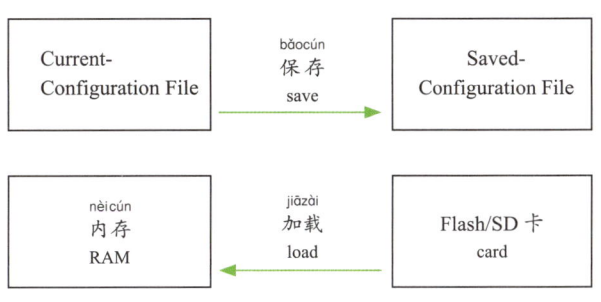

```
┌──────────────┐    bǎocún    ┌──────────────┐
│  Current-    │   保 存      │  Saved-      │
│ Configuration│ ──────────▶  │ Configuration│
│    File      │    save      │    File      │
└──────────────┘              └──────────────┘

┌──────────────┐   jiāzài     ┌──────────────┐
│   nèicún     │   加 载      │              │
│   内 存      │ ◀──────────  │  Flash/SD 卡 │
│   RAM        │    load      │    card      │
└──────────────┘              └──────────────┘
```

三、视听说

徒弟：手动保存每次都要输入命令，有没有简单点的方法？

师傅：有的，使用 set save-configuration interval 命令，如设置间隔 60 分钟系统在本地自动保存配置文件。

徒弟：如何把配置文件做一个备份？

师傅：文件的扩展名必须是 *.zip 或 *.cfg，用 save 后面接文件名。

徒弟：如何从存储器恢复配置文件？

师傅：（用）startup saved-configuration 命令。

<Huawei>startup saved-configuration config.zip

四、学以致用

小机器人：现在实际操作如何查看配置和处理文件系统异常情况吧。

（1）用 display current-configuration 命令，查看当前配置。

    <Huawei>display current-configuration

（2）用 display saved-configuration 命令，查看保存的配置文件。

    <Huawei>display saved-configuration

（3）当存储设备的文件系统出现异常时，可以用 fixdisk 命令修复。

    <Huawei>fixdisk flash:

（4）存储设备格式化，格式化会导致数据丢失。

    <Huawei>format flash:

第七单元　虚拟局域网

一、热身

小机器人：VLAN 是英文 Virtual Local Area Network 的简称，又叫虚拟局域网，是一种通过将局域网内的设备从逻辑上划分为一个个网段，从而实现虚拟工作组的技术。与传统的局域网技术相比，虚拟局域网更具灵活性和安全稳定性；且能减少管理开销、节约成本；网络带宽利用率更高；能够帮助实现网络访问控制功能和信息系统的无忧共享。

三、视听说

小机器人：一起来划分 VLAN 并进行划分前后的效果验证。这里是单台交换机接 4 台电脑，可以看到，不划分 VLAN 时，电脑间的连通情况。在不划分 VLAN 时，每台 PC 设一个 IP，相互都能 Ping 通，显示单台交换机的 VLAN 号，显示 4 台计算机都在同一个 VLAN。计算机名为 PC1、PC2、PC3、PC4。按此图在 eNSP（Enterprise Network Simulation Platform）中先把 4 台计算机 IP 地址设好，并使它们相互能 Ping 通，但划分 VLAN 之后就不一样了。

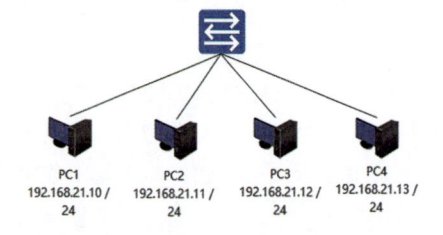

PC1 192.168.21.10 / 24　　PC2 192.168.21.11 / 24　　PC3 192.168.21.12 / 24　　PC4 192.168.21.13 / 24

四、学以致用

小机器人：单台交换机接 4 台电脑，不划分 VLAN 时，电脑间相互能 Ping 通。现在，我们设置虚拟子网，将 PC1 和 PC3 设置在同一个子网，把 PC2 和 PC4 设置在同一个子网，再来看他们的互通情况。可以看到，PC1 和 PC3 相互能 Ping 通，因为它们在同一个子网。PC2 和 PC3 相互不能 Ping 通，因为它们不在同一个子网。

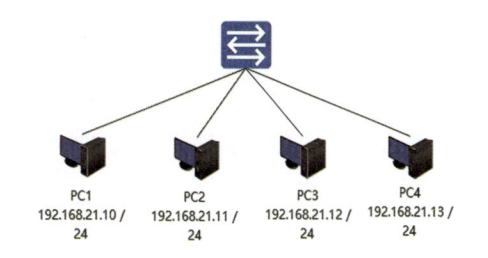

第八单元　IP 地址与子网掩码

一、热身

徒弟：子网掩码的长度是什么意思？

师傅：首先把子网掩码从点分十进制表示为二进制，然后看高位有多少个"1"，子网掩码的长度就有多少位。

徒弟：那十进制如何转换成二进制呢？

师傅：用计算机自带的计算器就可以计算出来了。

徒弟：能举个例子吗？

师傅：比如 255.255.255.240 表示为二进制就是：11111111.11111111.11111111.11110000，从高位往低位数，一共有 28 个"1"，所以该子网掩码的长度就是 28 位。

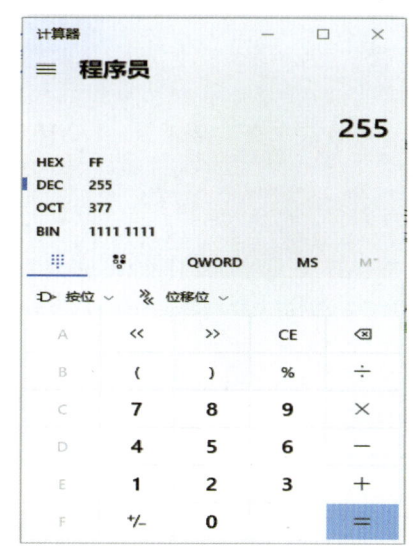

三、视听说

徒弟：如何计算 IP 地址所在网络的网络地址？

师傅：如果将一个子网掩码与一个IP地址进行逐位"与"运算，所得的结果便是该IP地址所在网络的网络地址。看下面这个例子：

	第一字节	第二字节	第三字节	第四字节
IP 地址	11010010	00011100	01100100	00001010
子网掩码	11111111	11111111	11111111	00000000
逐位相"与"运算结果	11010010	00011100	01100100	00000000
网络地址	210	28	100	0

四、学以致用

徒弟：如何判断两个 IP 地址是否在同一个子网内？

师傅：那先要分别计算一下两个 IP 地址各自的网络地址，如果两个 IP 地址所在网络的网络地址相同，就说明它们在同一个子网内。

149

徒弟：是将 IP 地址与其对应的子网掩码进行逐位"与"运算，来计算该 IP 地址所在网络的网络地址吧？
师傅：对的。让我们一起来算一下这两个 IP 地址所在网络的网络地址，看看它们是否相同。

第九单元　用路由器组建网络

一、热身

徒弟：静态路由配置包括哪些步骤？
师傅：第一步，下载并安装 eNSP 软件。
　　　第二步，打开 eNSP 软件，绘制网络拓扑图。
　　　第三步，启动所需设备。
　　　第四步，打开路由器模拟器，进行静态路由配置。
　　　第五步，打开计算机模拟器，设置 IP 地址、子网掩码和网关。
　　　第六步，保存配置，并测试计算机连通性。

三、视听说

A：私有地址和公有地址的区别是什么？
B：私有地址就是在 A、B、C 三类 IP 地址中保留下来为企业内部网络分配地址时所使用的 IP 地址。私有地址主要用于在局域网中进行分配，在 Internet 上是无效的。必须通过 NAT 将内部 IP 地址转换成公网上可用的 IP 地址。
A：我知道 A、B、C 类公有地址范围，那私有地址范围呢？
B：这是 A 类私有地址范围：10.0.0.0~10.255.255.255。这是 B 类私有地址范围：172.16.0.0~172.31.255.255。这是 C 类私有地址范围：192.168.0.0~192.168.255.255。

四、学以致用

小机器人：将 R1 和 R2 相连接的两个端口的 IP 地址分别设置为 192.168.21.1/30、192.168.21.2/30。R1 连接 S1 的端口 IP 地址设置为 192.168.20.1/24，R2 连接 S2 的端口，IP 地址设置为 192.168.22.1/24。观察 4 台电脑与 S1 和 S2 相互通讯时的 IP 地址的设置是什么。

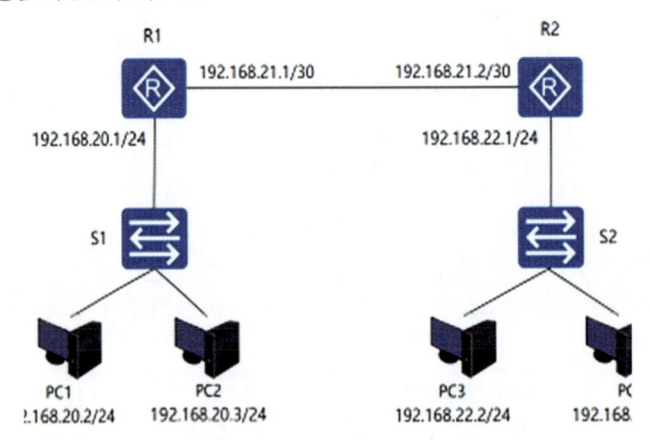

第十单元　IP 地址管理

一、热身

DHCP 的基本工作流程分为四个阶段，即发现阶段、提供阶段、请求阶段和确认阶段。其中，发现阶段对应 DHCPDISCOVER 消息，提供阶段对应 DHCPOFFER 消息，请求阶段对应 DHCPREQUEST 消息，确认阶段对应 DHCPACK/ DHCPNACK 消息。

三、视听说

师傅：地址池创建方式主要有两种：接口地址池和全局地址池。

徒弟：两种地址池创建方式有什么区别呢？

师傅：接口地址池内的 IP 地址与此接口的 IP 地址属于同一网段，且地址池中地址只能分配给此接口下的客户端；全局地址池中地址可以分配给设备所有接口下的客户端。

四、学以致用

小机器人：开启基于接口地址池的 DHCP 服务器功能的操作步骤：

第一步，执行命令 system-view，进入系统视图；第二步，执行命令 interface interface-type interface-number，进入接口视图；第三步，执行命令 ip address ip-address { mask | mask-length }，配置接口的 IP 地址；第四步，执行命令 dhcp select interface，开启接口地址池的 DHCP 服务器功能。

参考答案 Reference Answers

第一单元

一、热身

1. ①C ②F ③A ④E ⑤D ⑥B
2. ①E ②A ③B ④C ⑤D

三、视听说

1. ①B ②A ③D ④C

四、学以致用

①D ②B ③C ④A

第二单元

一、热身

1. ①A ②B
2. ①B ②A

三、视听说

1. ①A ②B ③C ④D ⑤E ⑥F

四、学以致用

①B ②A ③D ④C ⑤F ⑥E

第三单元

一、热身

1. ①E ②C ③A ④B ⑤F ⑥D
2. ①B ②C ③A

三、视听说

1. ①B ②D

四、学以致用

①C ②D ③A

第四单元

一、热身

1. ①B ②A
2. ①B ②A ③D ④C

三、视听说

1. ①B ②A ③E ④C ⑤D

四、学以致用

①F ②E ③C ④D ⑤A ⑥B

第五单元

一、热身

1. ①C ②D ③F ④B ⑤A ⑥E
2. ①A ②BC ③BD ④A

三、视听说

1. ①D ②B ③A ④C

四、学以致用

①B ②A ③D ④C

第六单元

一、热身

1. ①D ②A ③B ④E ⑤F ⑥C
2. ①BDF ②ACE

三、视听说

1. ①C ②A ③B

四、学以致用

①B ②C

第七单元

一、热身

1. A B C D E F
2. A B C D E F

三、视听说

1. 互通的

四、学以致用

①可以　A
②不可以　B
③不可以　B

第八单元

一、热身

1. A、B、E、F
2. ①D ②C ③A ④B

三、视听说

1. ①A ②B ③C ④D

四、学以致用

① 10101000　② 00010101　③ 0
④ 11000000　⑤ 00000000　⑥ 168

第九单元

一、热身

1.①C ②D ③B ④A ⑤F ⑥E
2.①C ②D ③E ④A ⑤B

三、视听说

1.①B ②C ③A

四、学以致用

①C ②D ③B ④A

第十单元

一、热身

1.①E ②D ③C ④B ⑤A ⑥F
2.①B ②D ③A ④C

三、视听说

1.①D ②B ③C ④A

四、学以致用

①D ②B ③A ④C